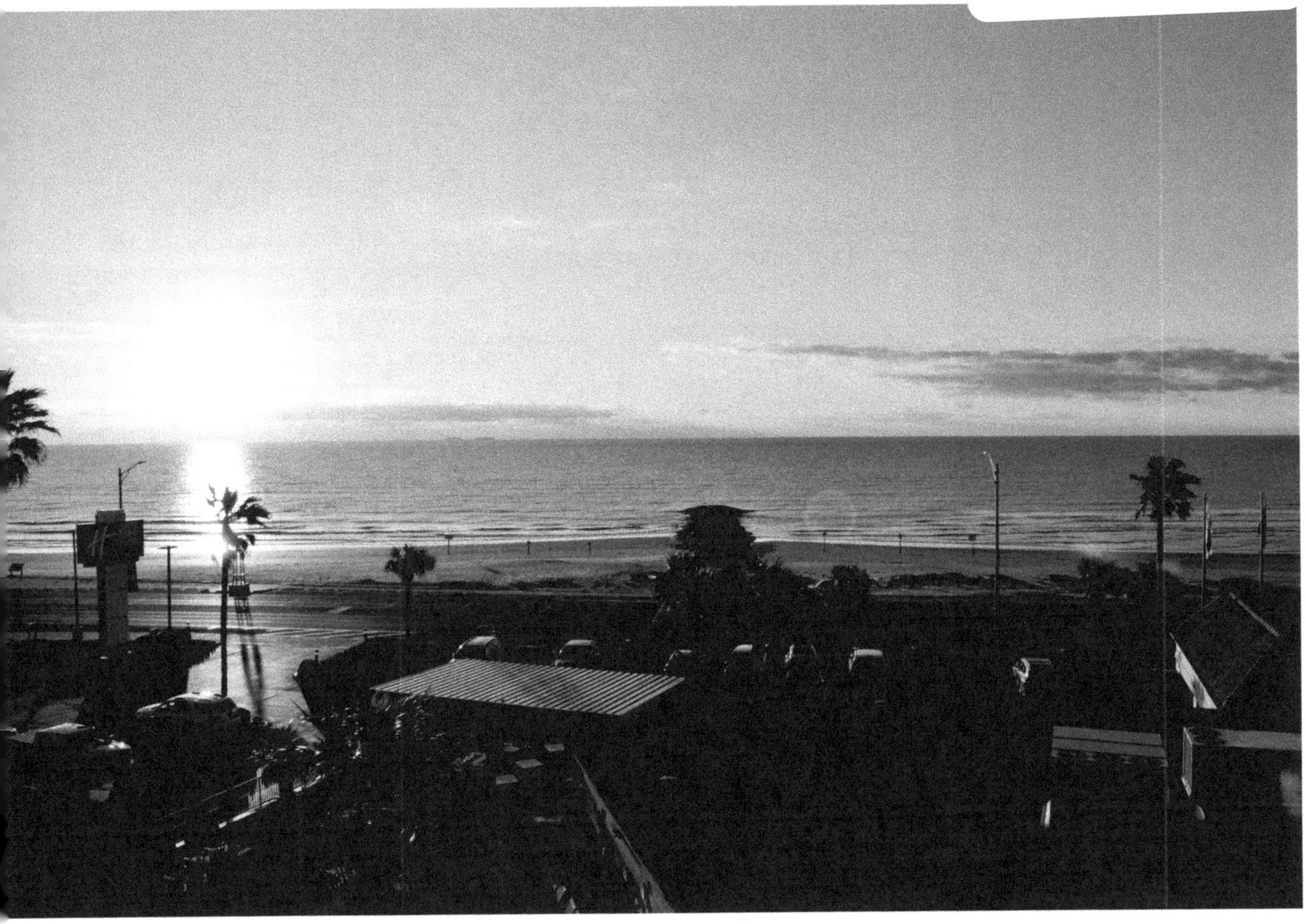

BY FRANCISCO JOSE ZANGEROLAME

GALVESTON TEXAS

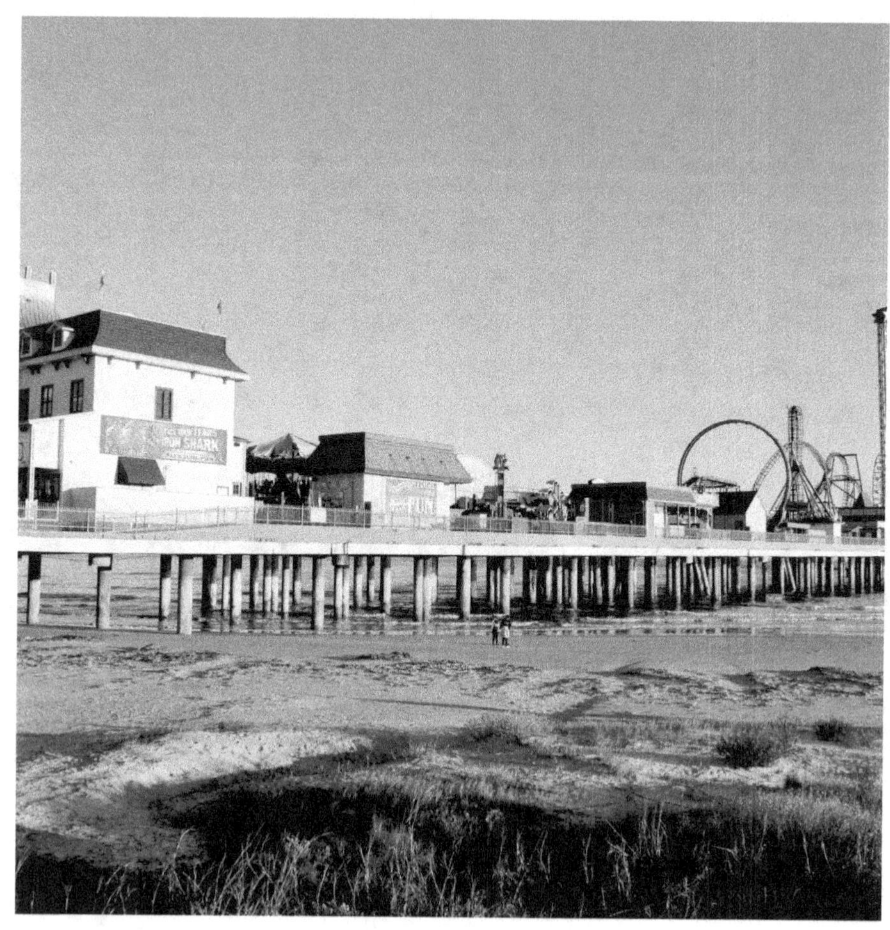

INSPIRED BY:

Cel Francisco and D. Apparecida Zangerolame

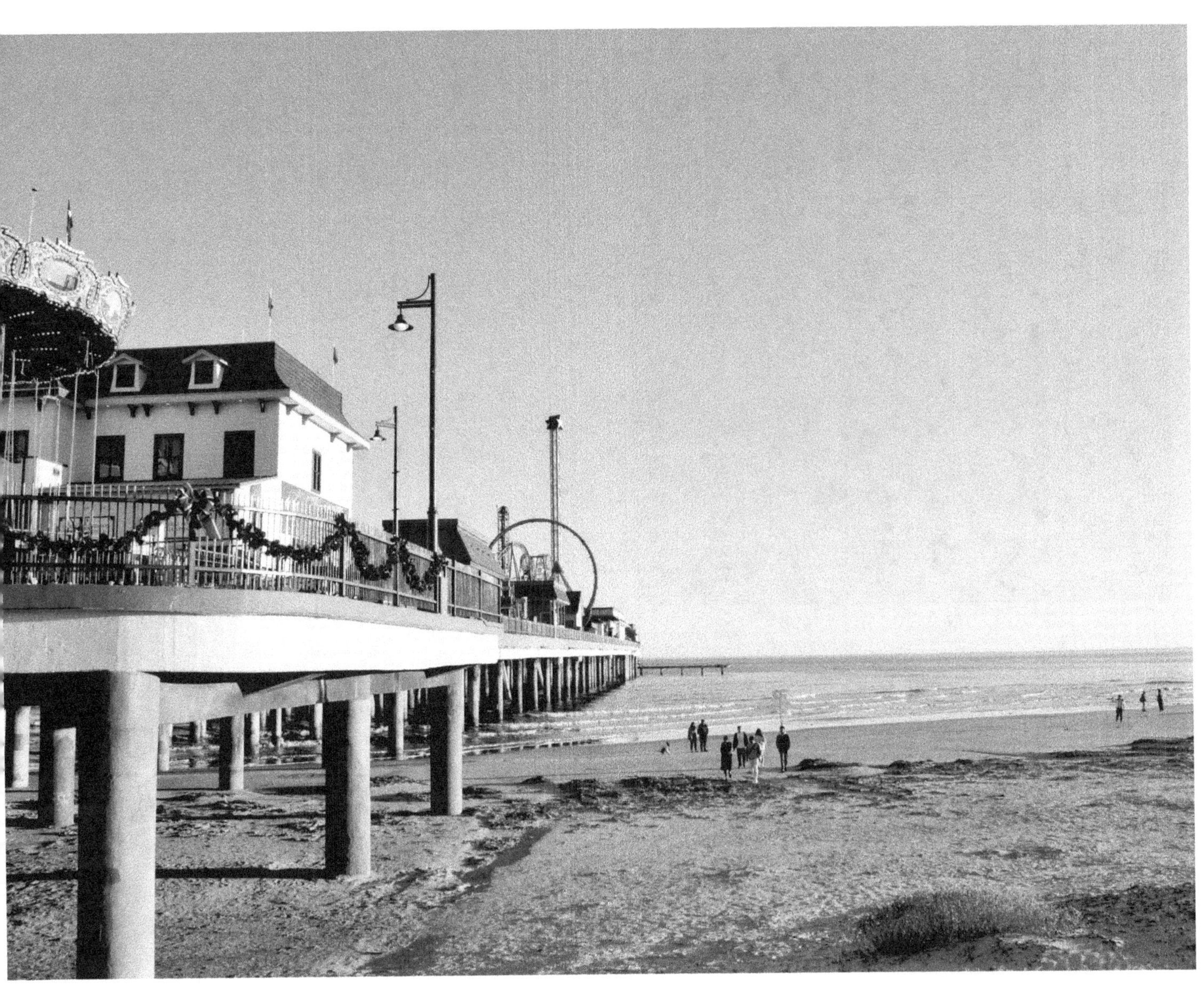

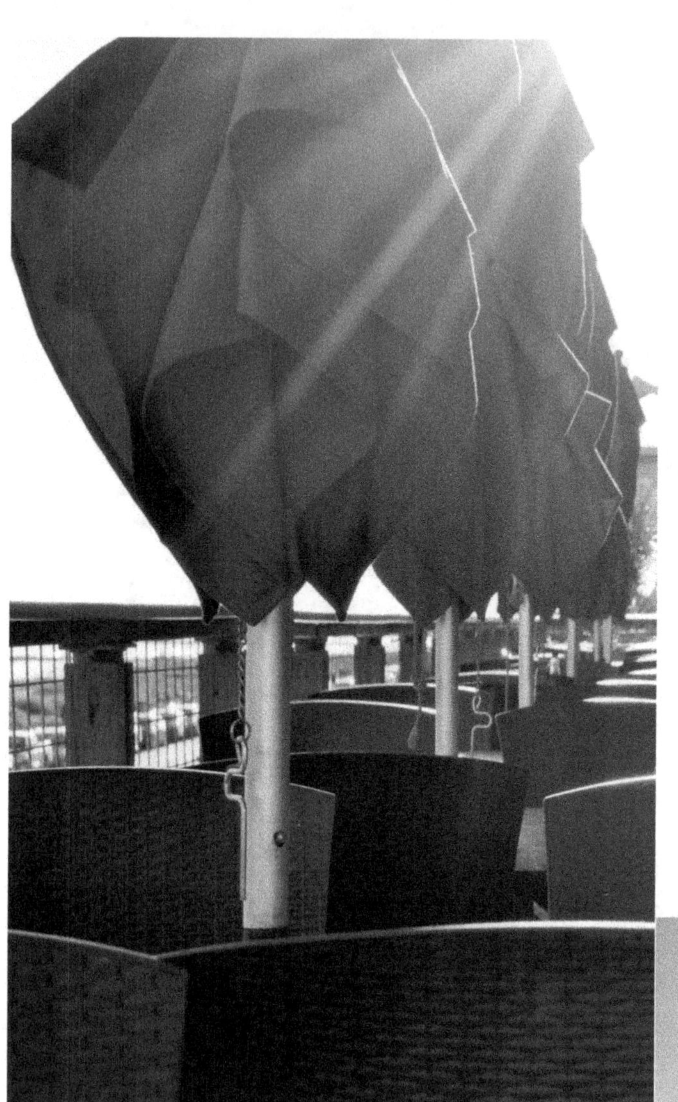

EMBRACE

Embrace the waves of change and let the tides of possibility carry you to new shores.

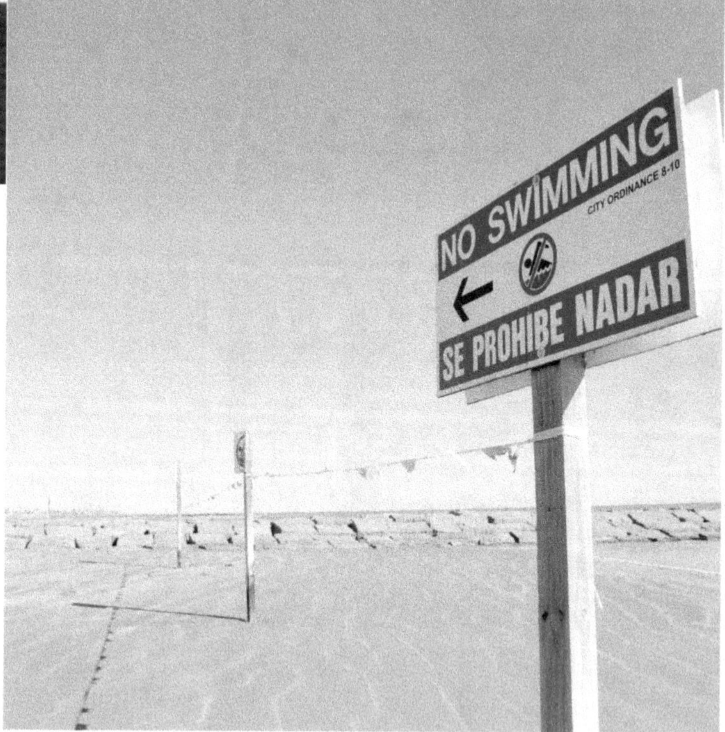

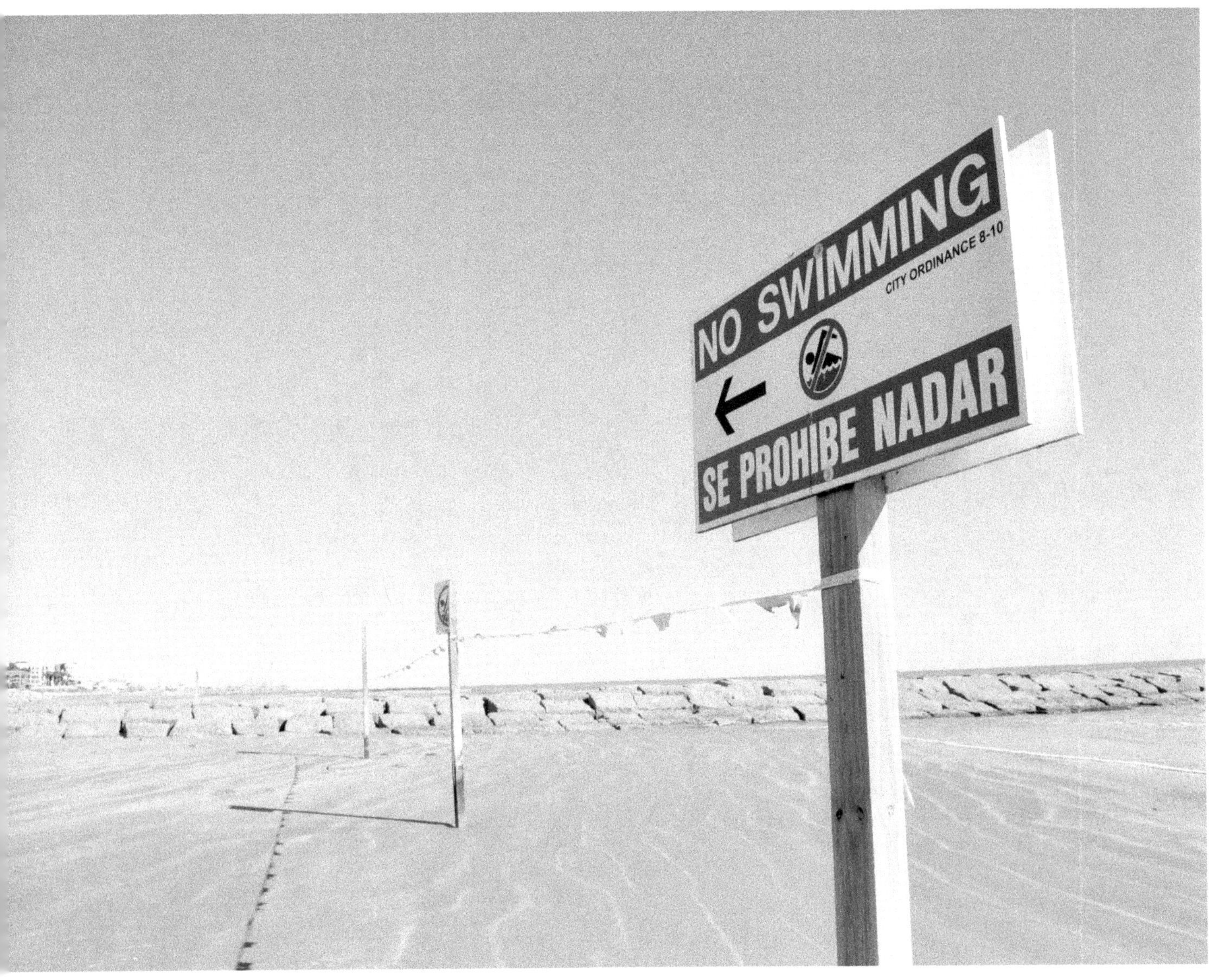

NO SWIMMING
CITY ORDINANCE 8-10
SE PROHIBE NADAR

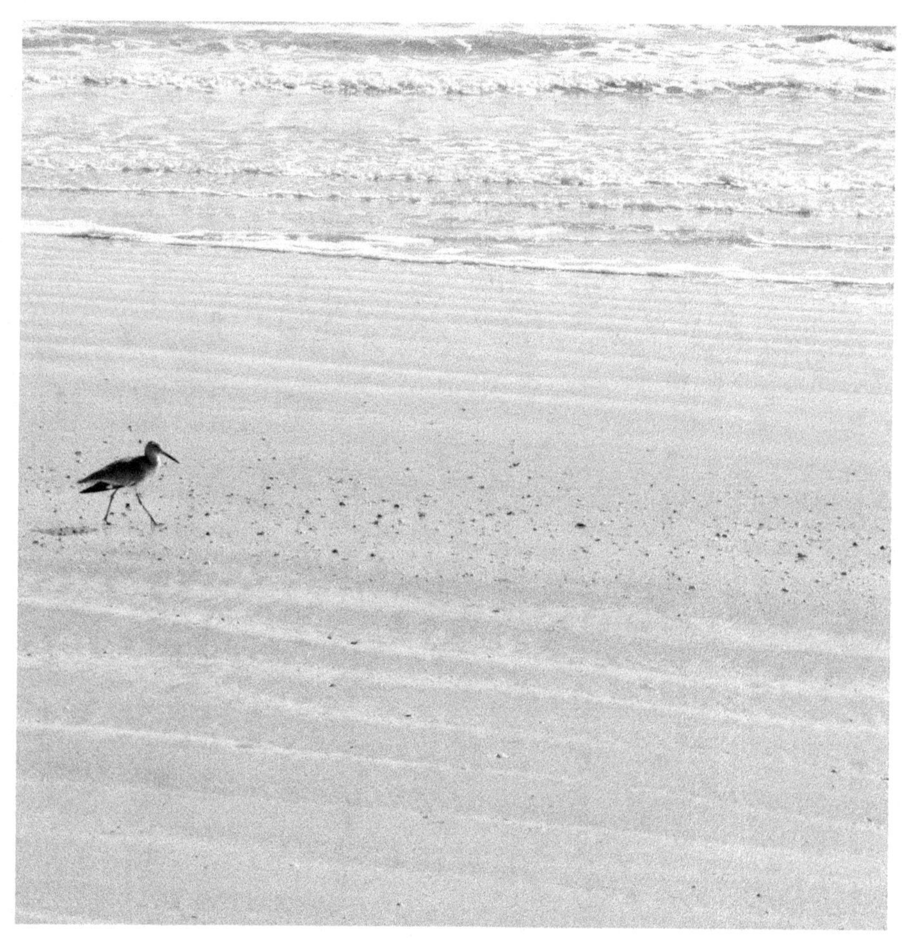

SUN, FUN & SAND

Life's a beach — find your perfect wave and ride it with joy.

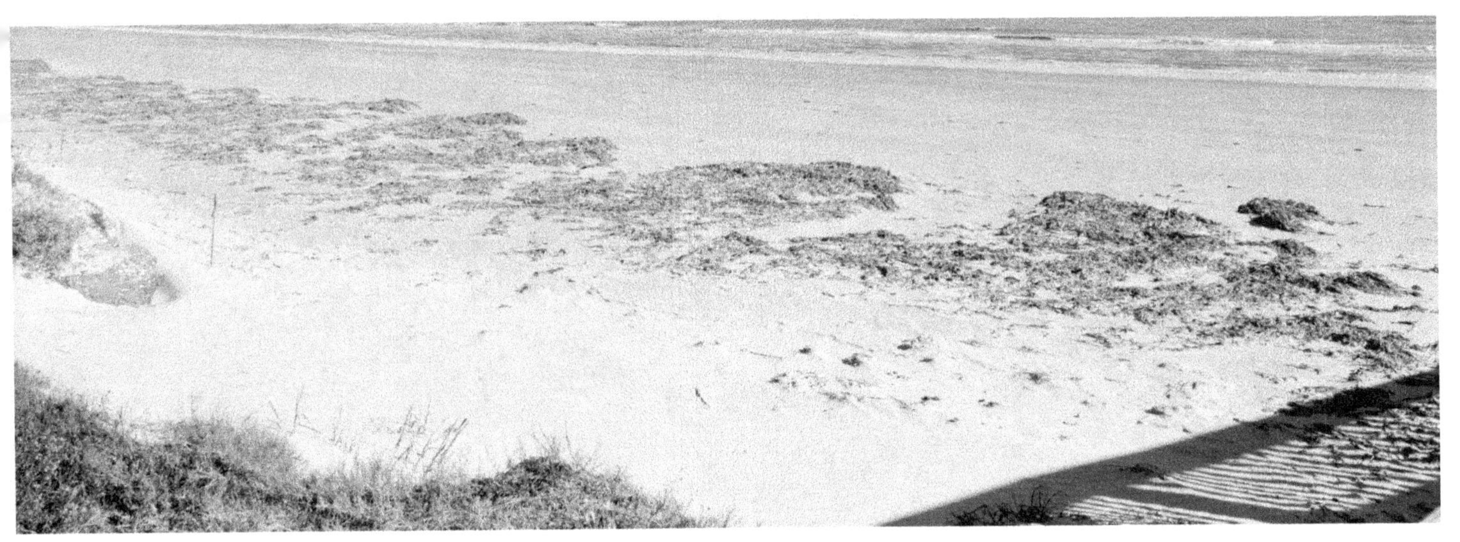

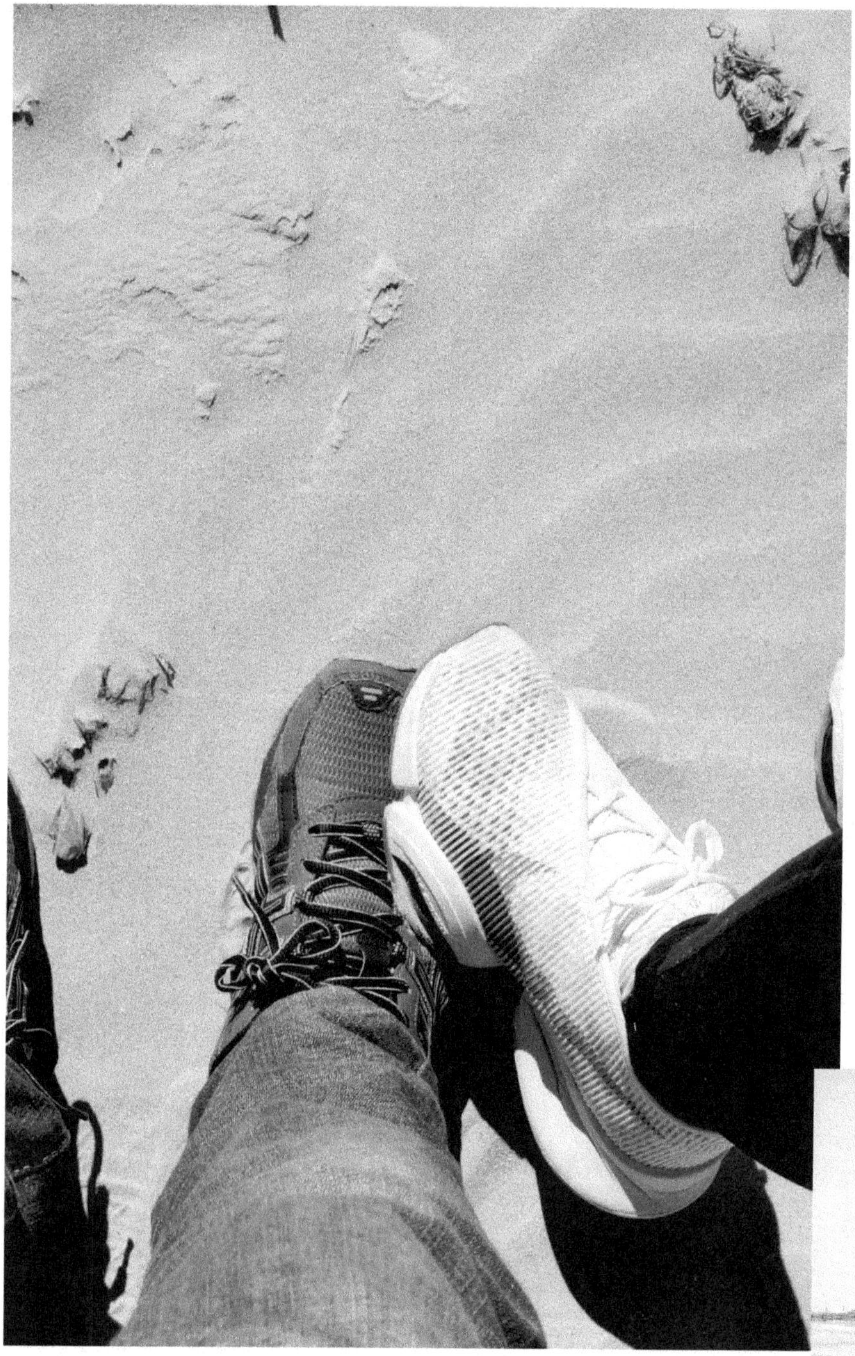

LOVE

*A day at the beach is a love letter to your soul,
signed by the sun, sea, and sand.*

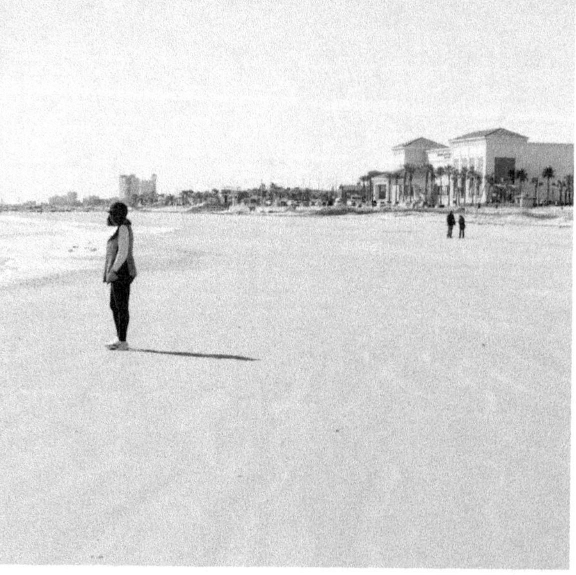

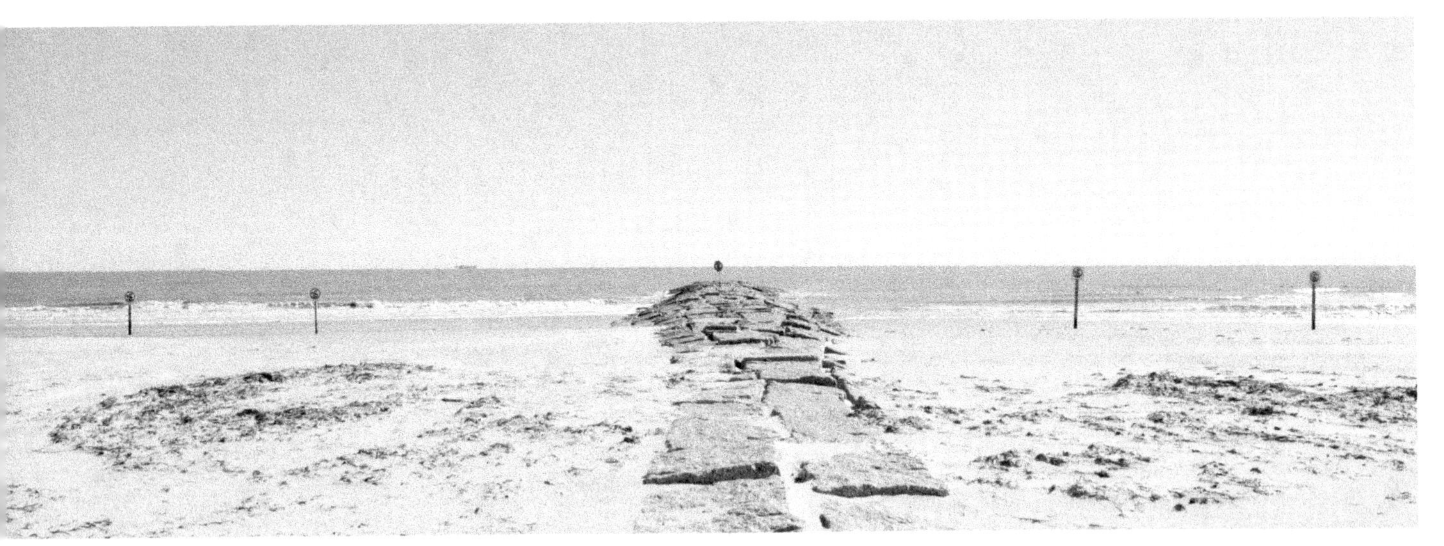

GRAIN...

*In every grain of sand, there is the story of the earth's journey. Find your story
in the sands of time.*

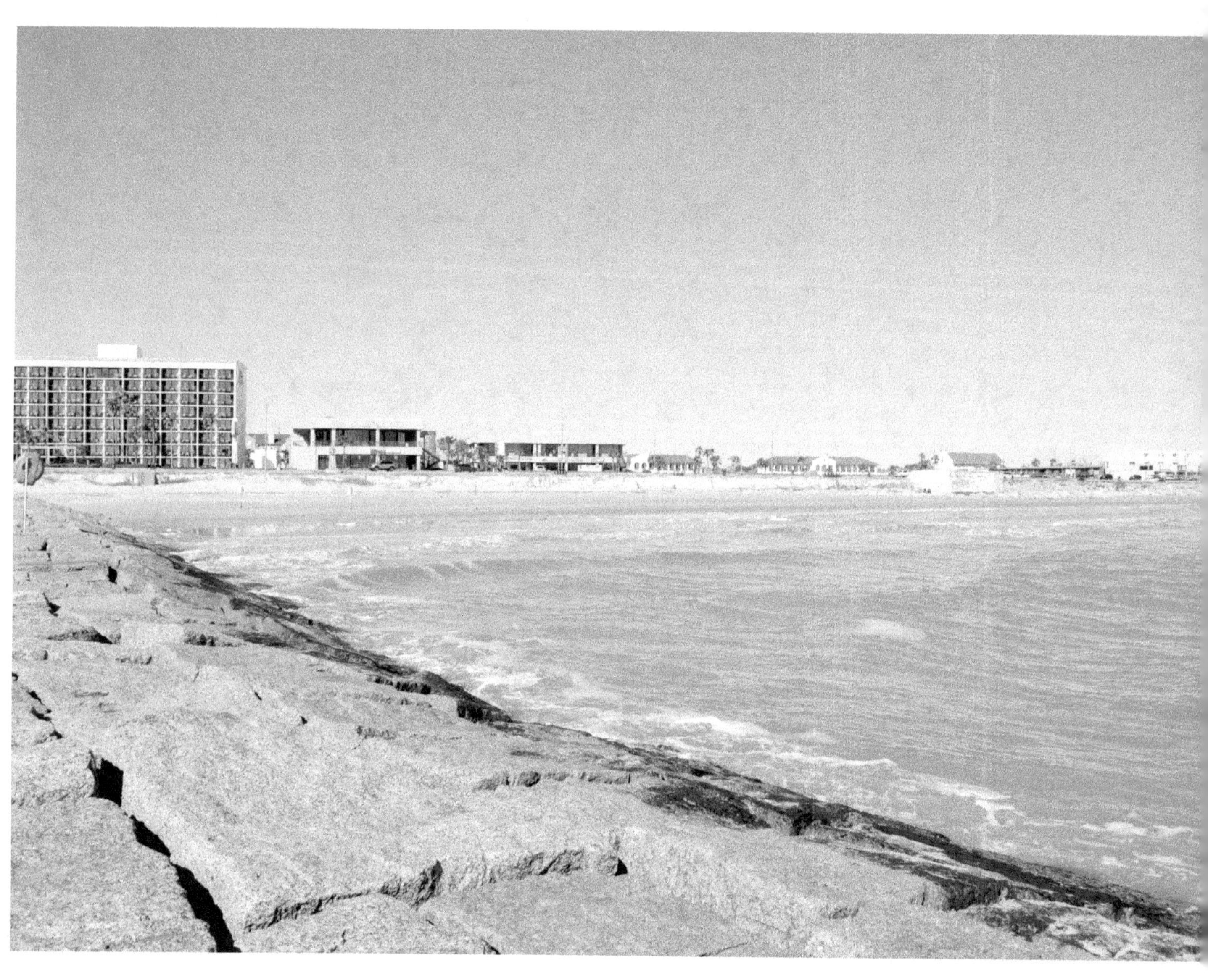

SEASHELLS

Seashells teach us that beauty often comes in small, simple packages.

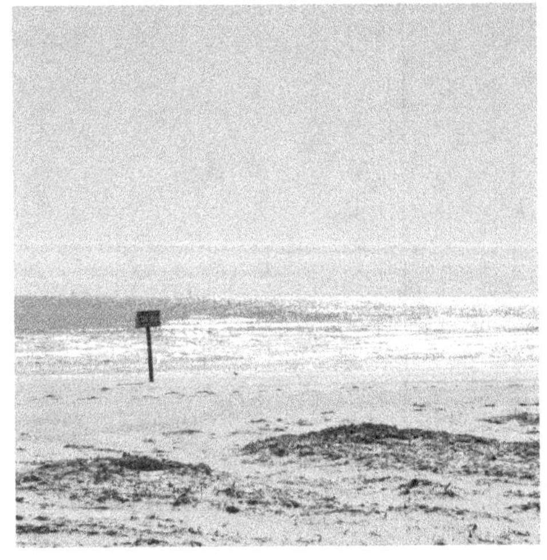

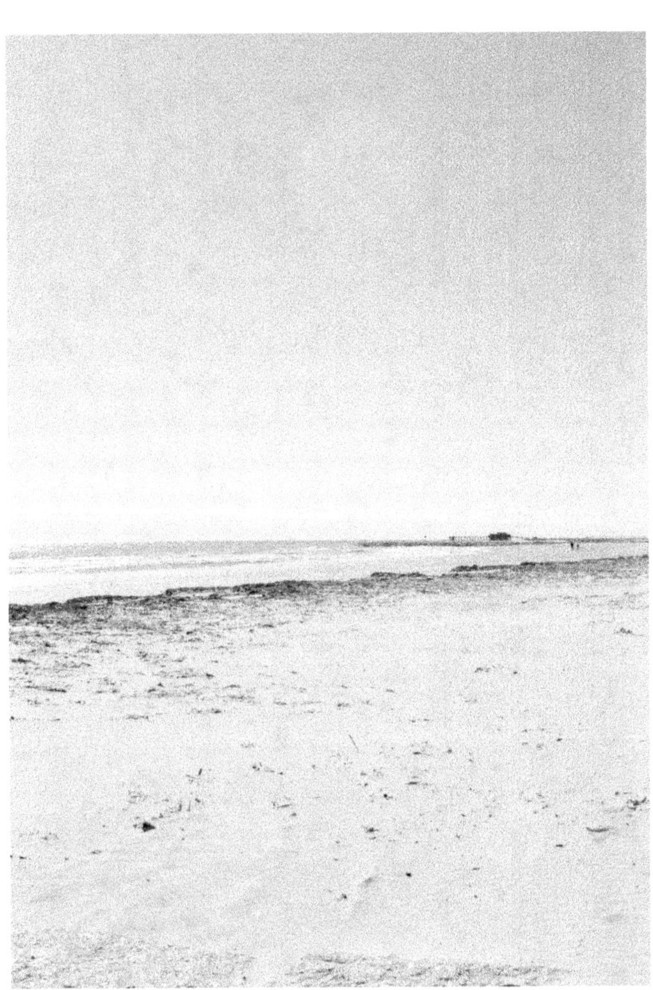

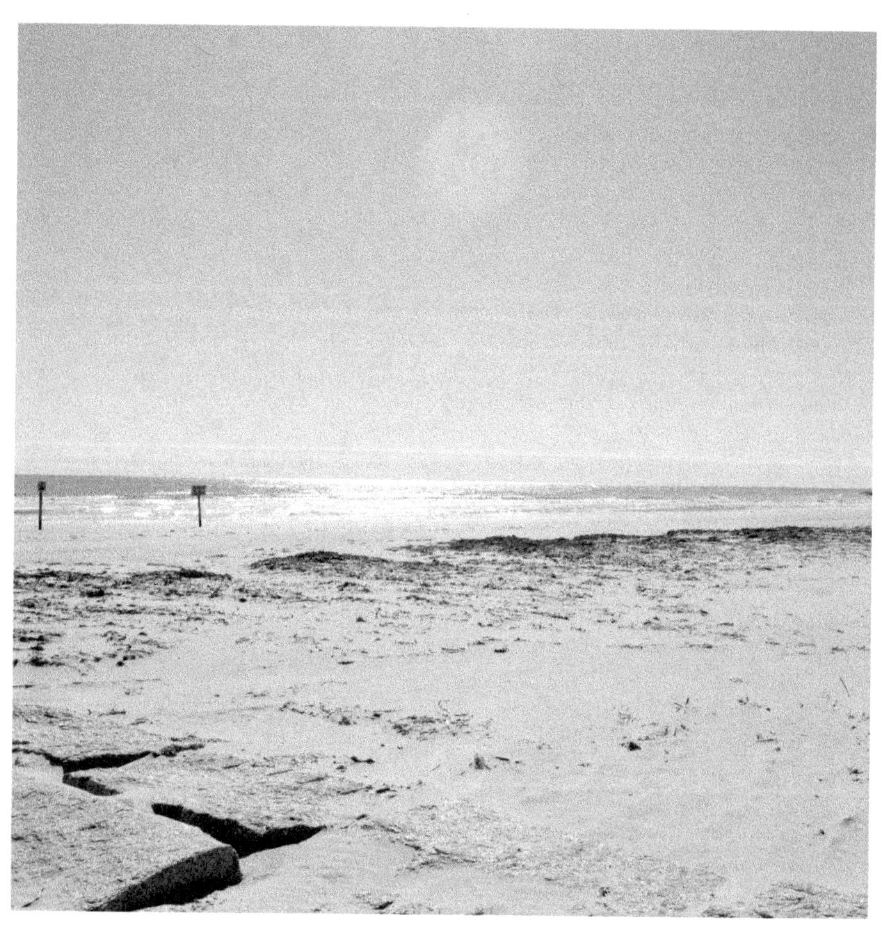

DANCE

Dance with the ocean, and let your worries drown in the rhythm of the waves.

The beach is nature's poetry, and the waves are its verses.

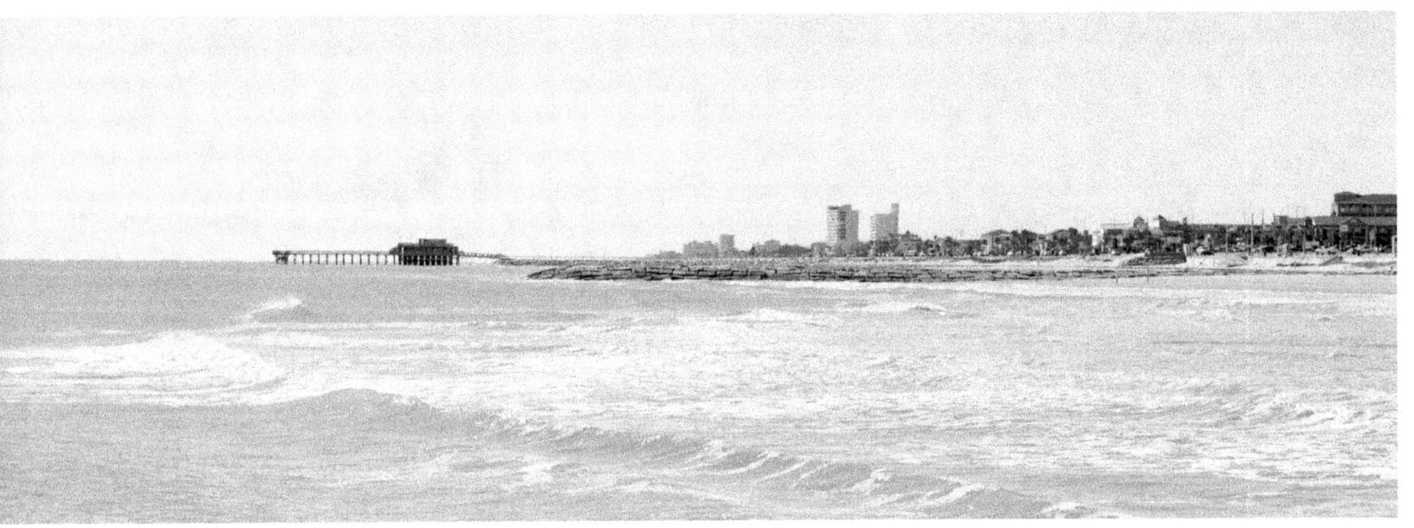

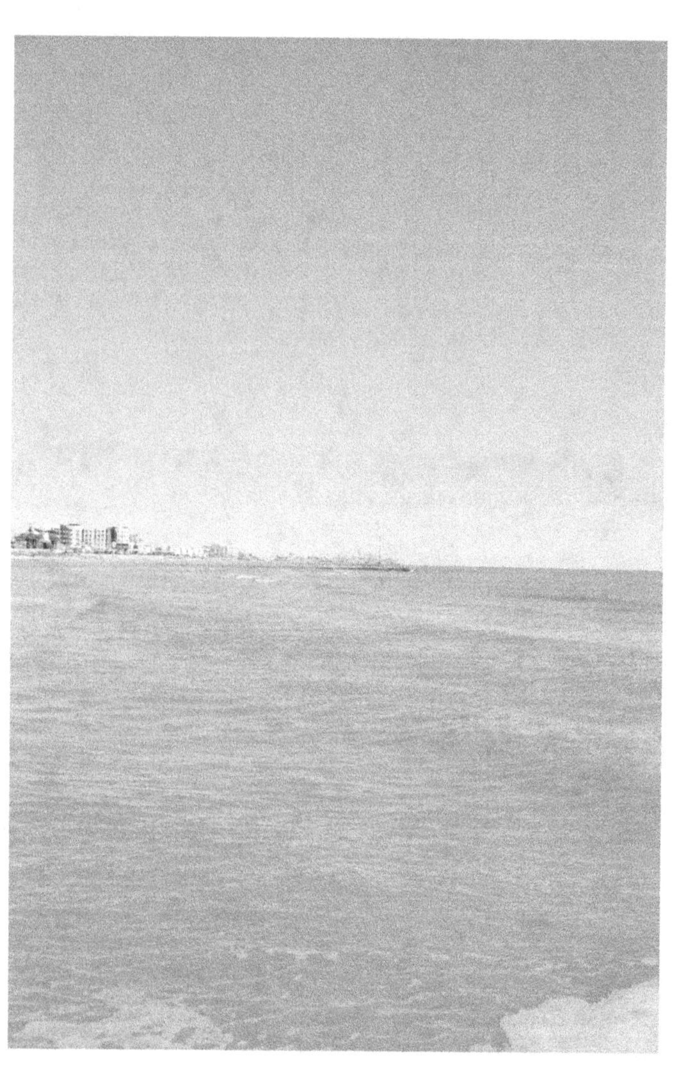

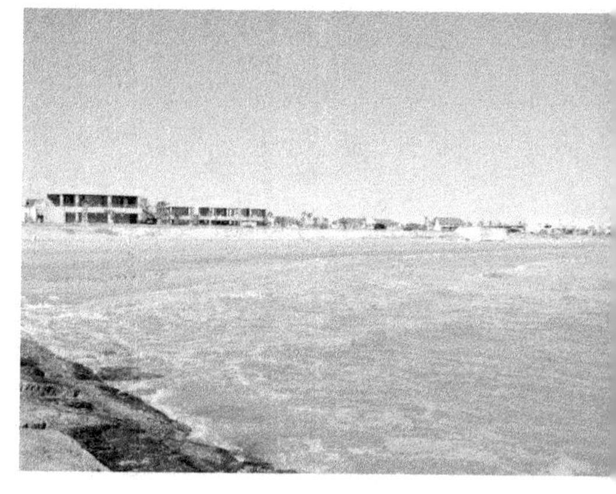

THE SHORE...

As the shore meets the sea, so do dreams meet reality.

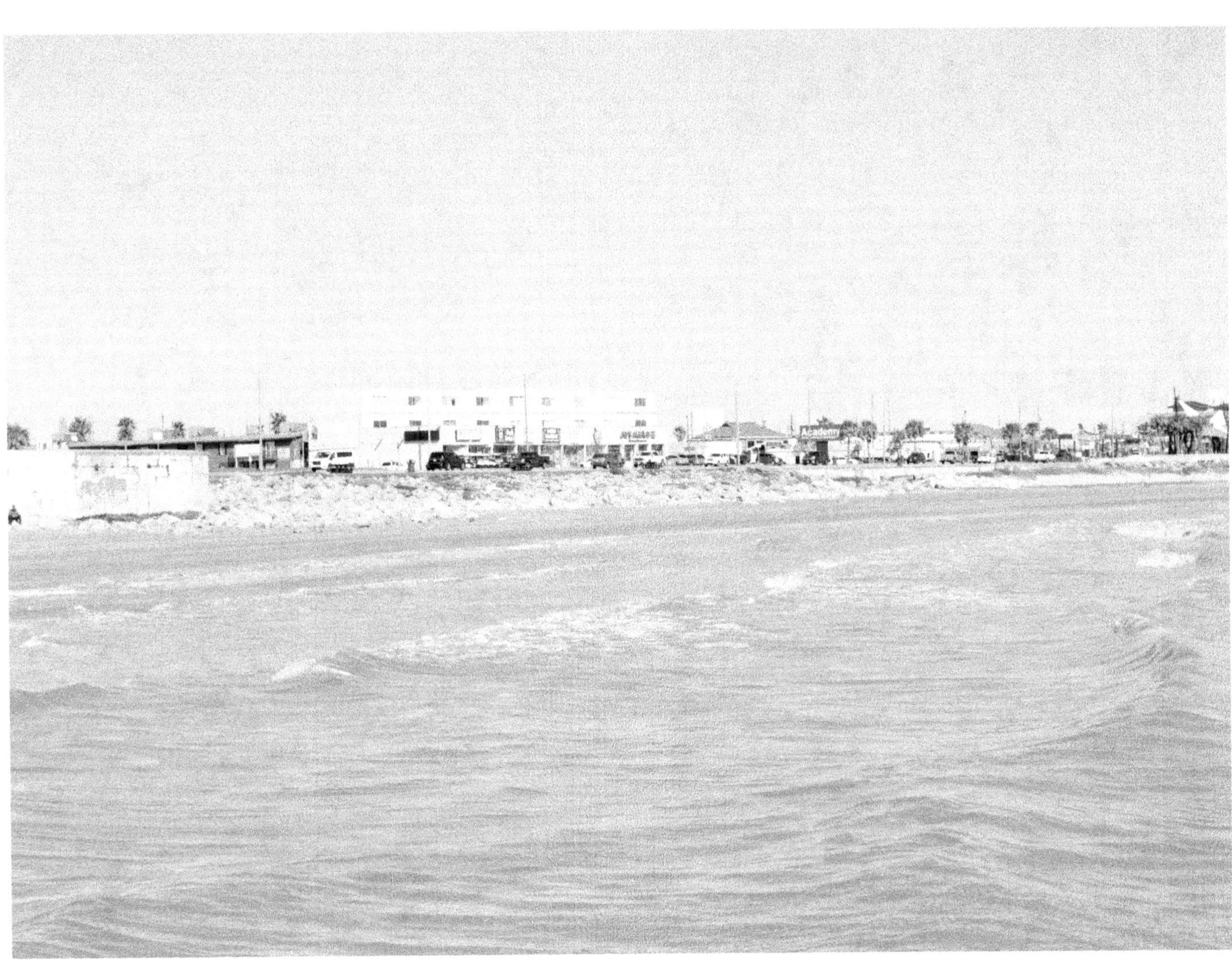

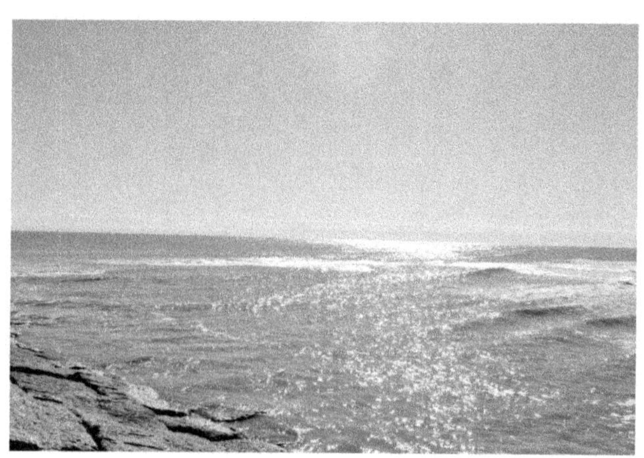

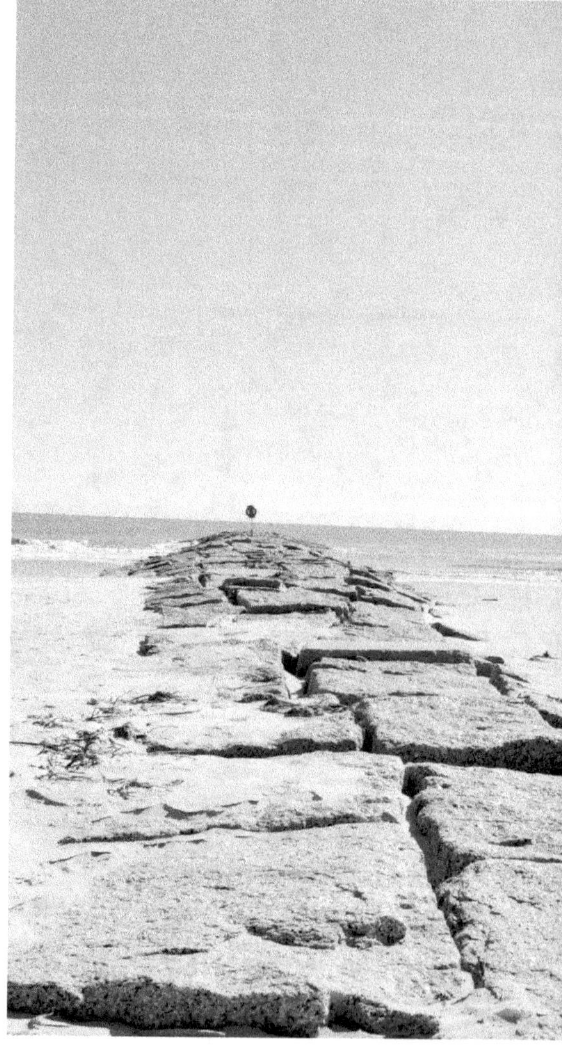

SUN-KISSED

Sun-kissed dreams and sandy toes – that's the recipe for a perfect day at the beach.

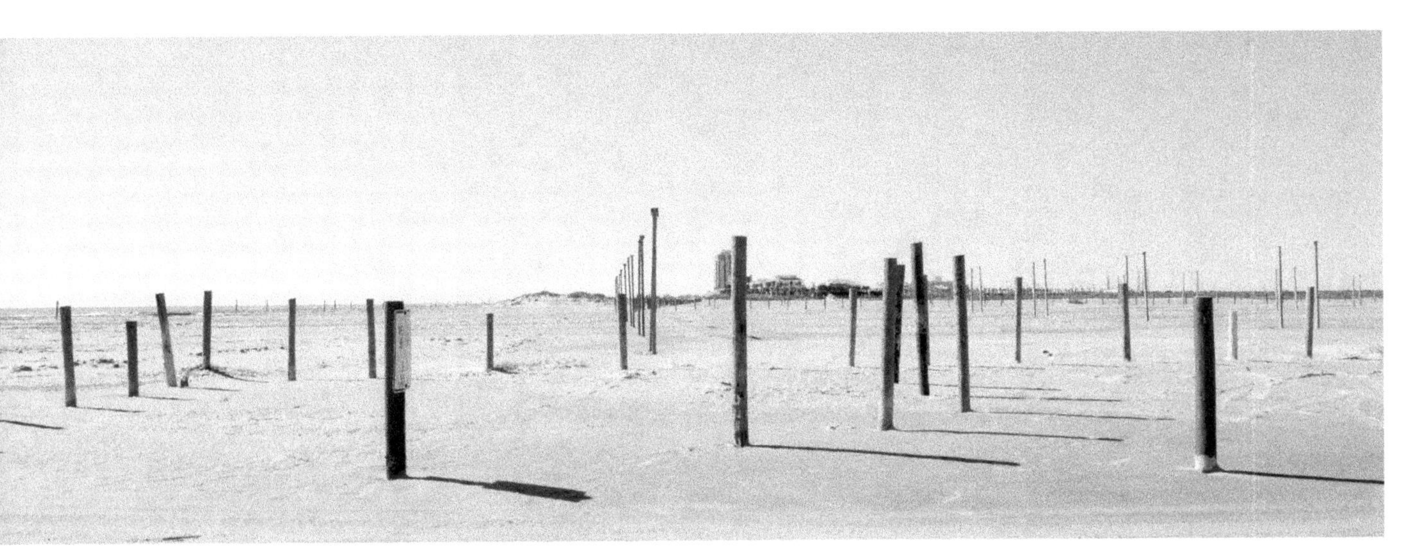

THE OCEAN...

The ocean is a reminder that, despite the chaos, there is always a calm within us.

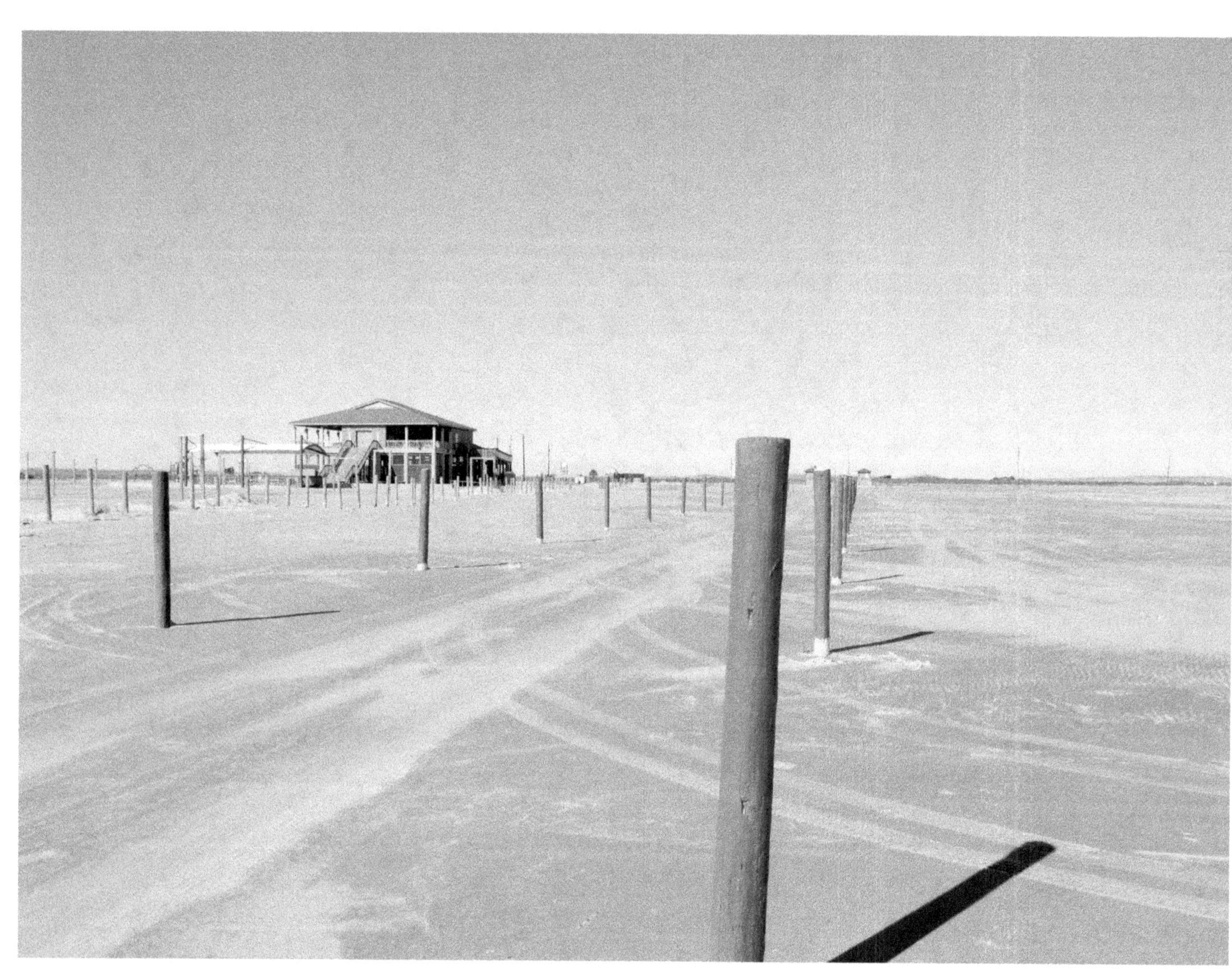

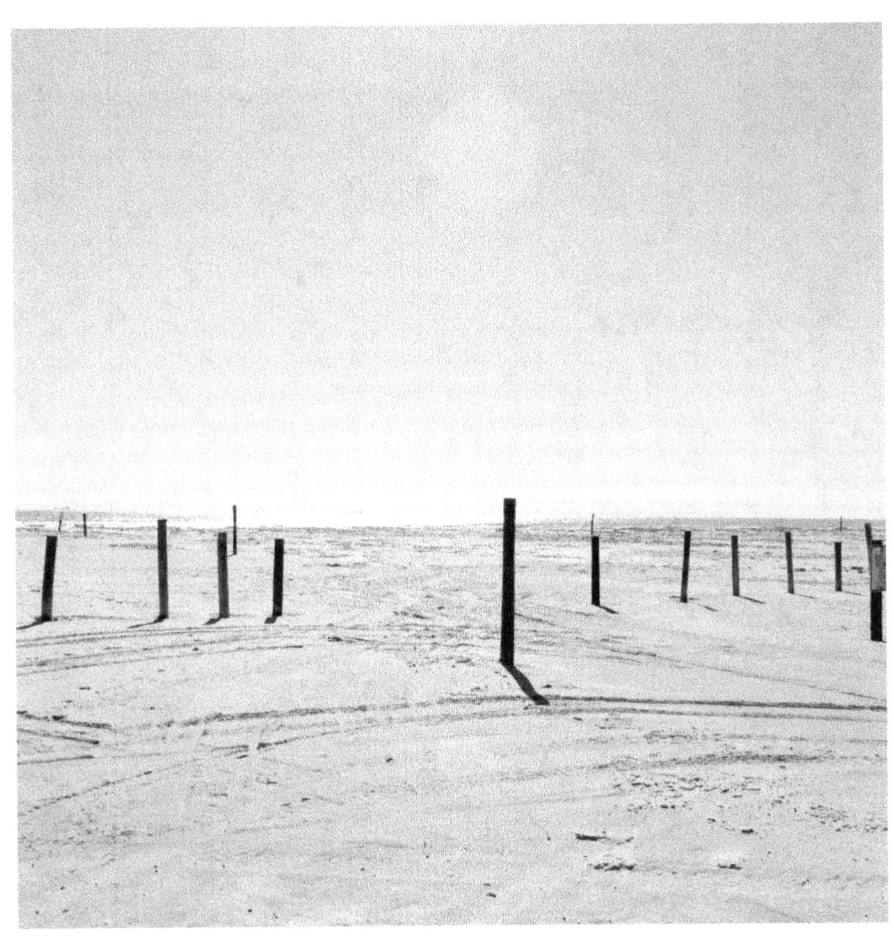

BUILD...

Build your castles in the sand, for dreams are the foundations of reality.

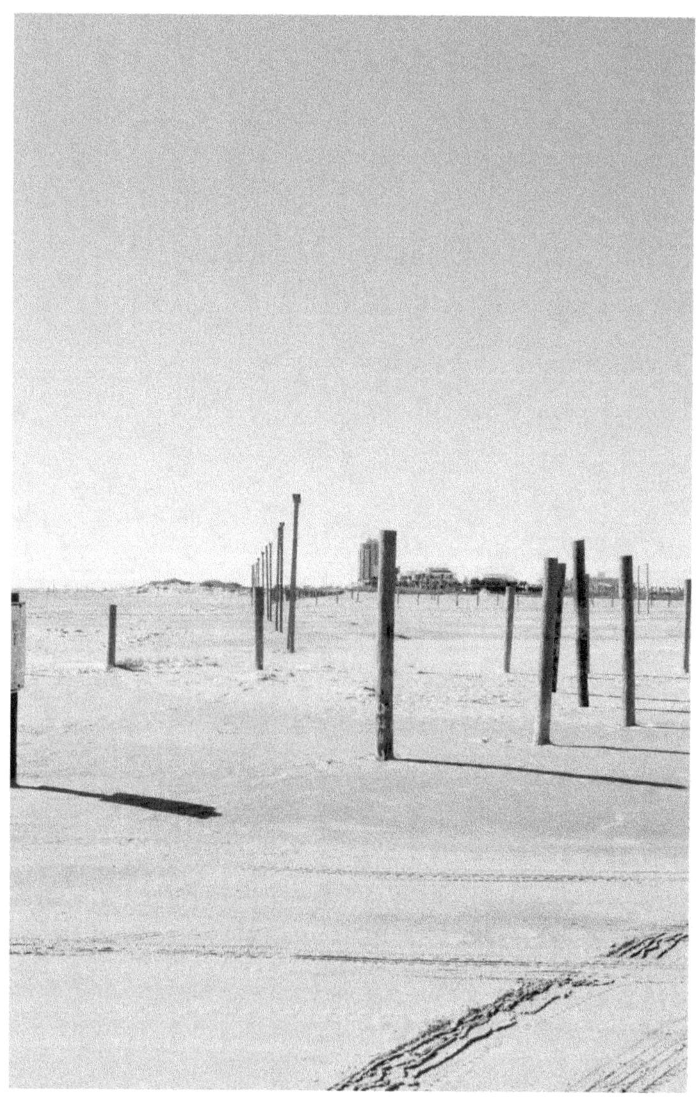

SANCTUARY

The beach is a sanctuary where the soul meets the sea, and the sun kisses the horizon.

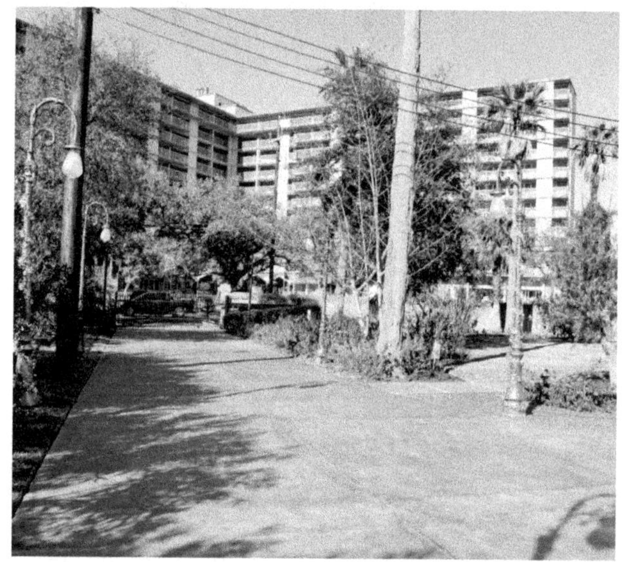

WAVES...

Let the rhythm of the waves be your heartbeat, and the beach your eternal dance floor.

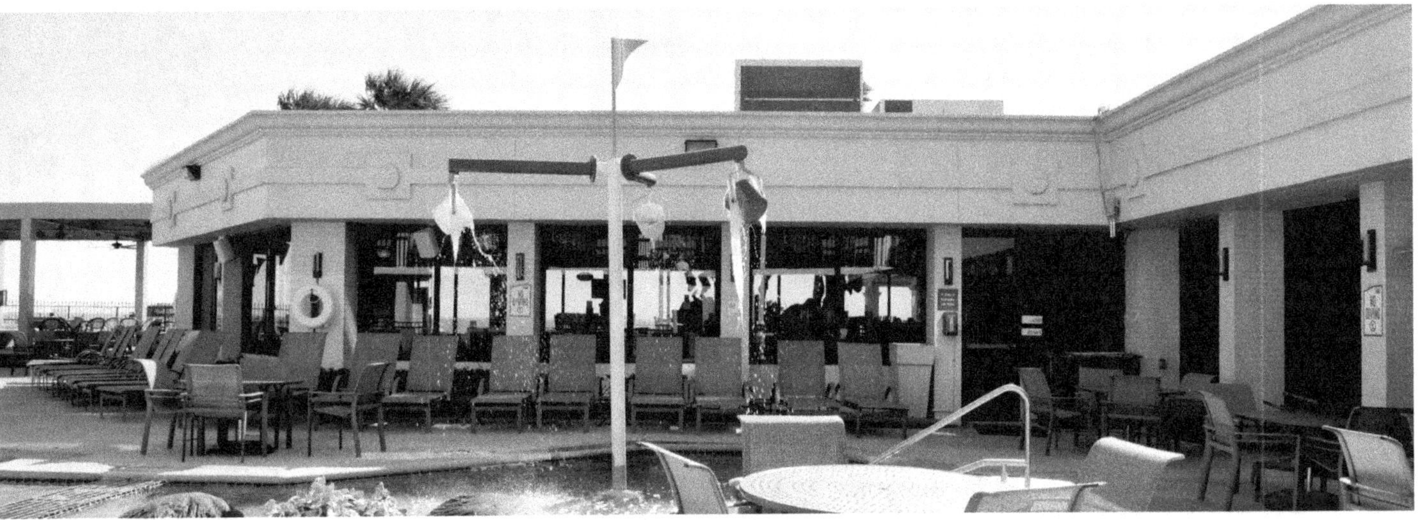

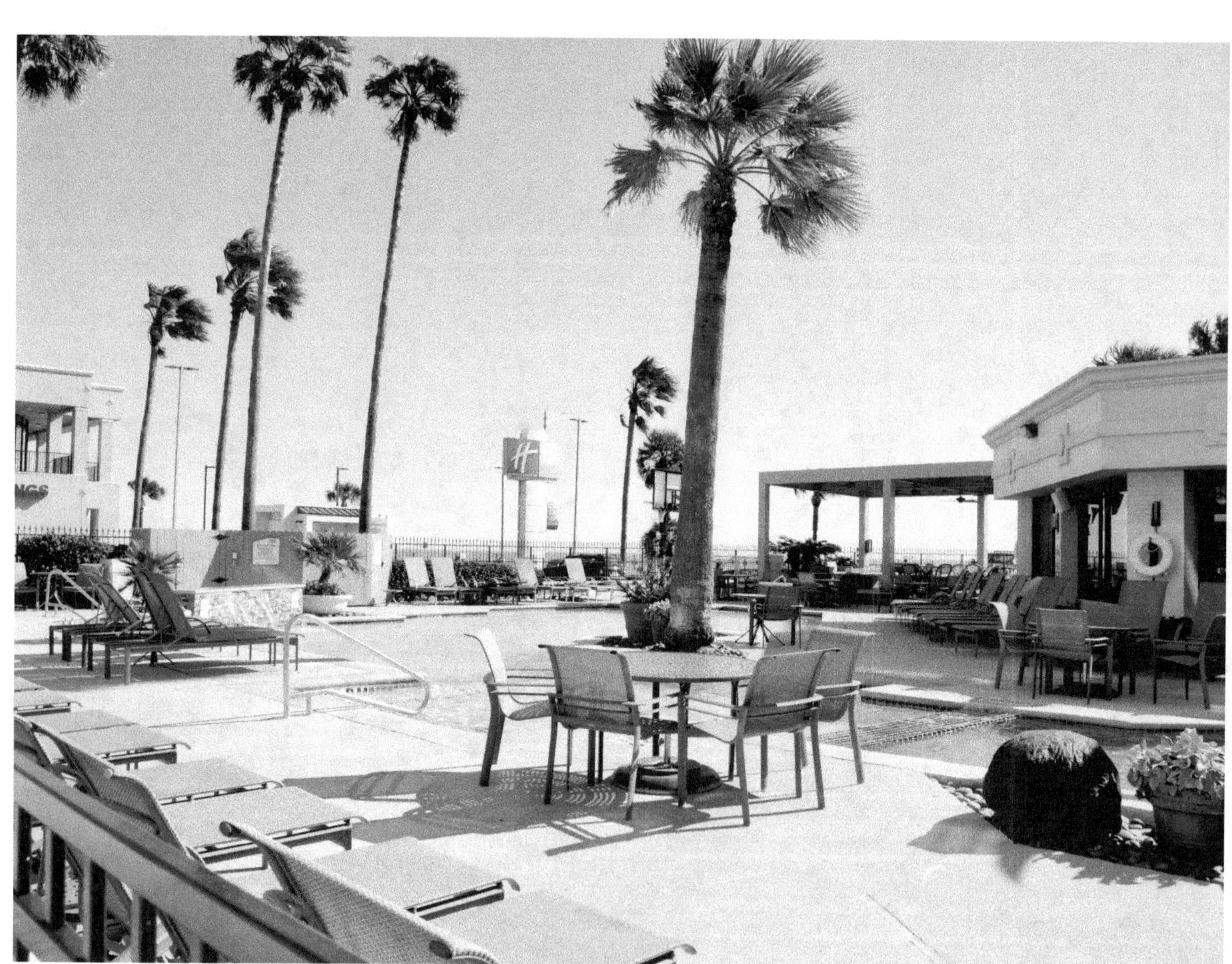

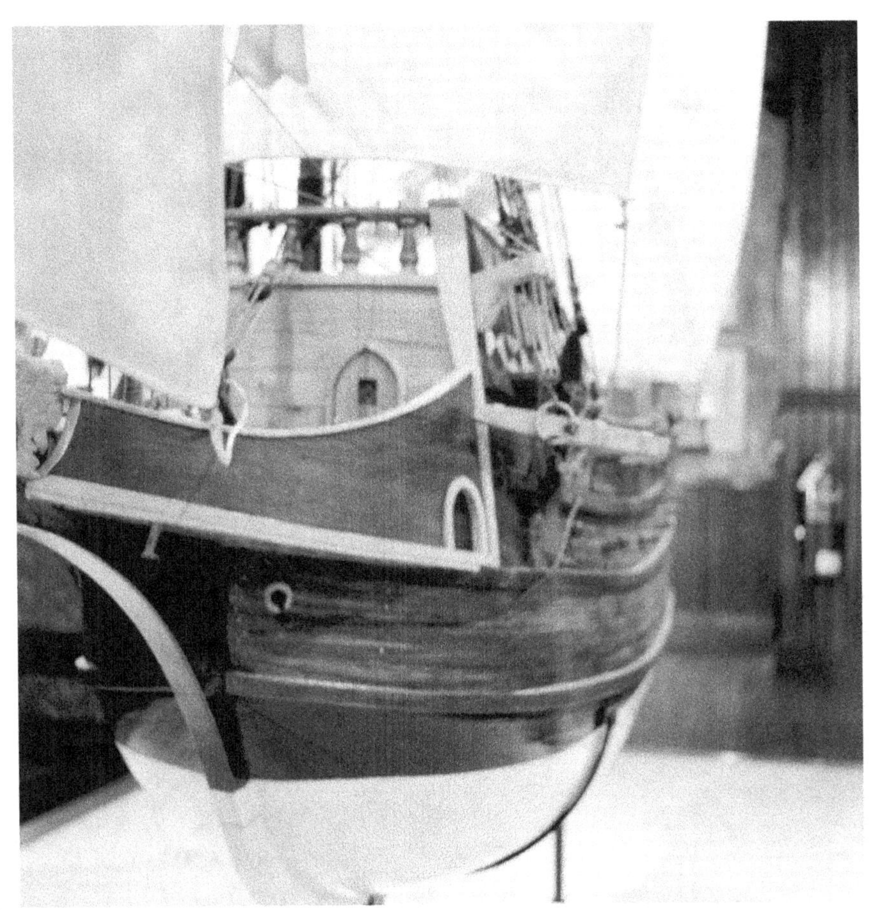

BEACH

The beach is a canvas painted with the hues of happiness – dive into the masterpiece

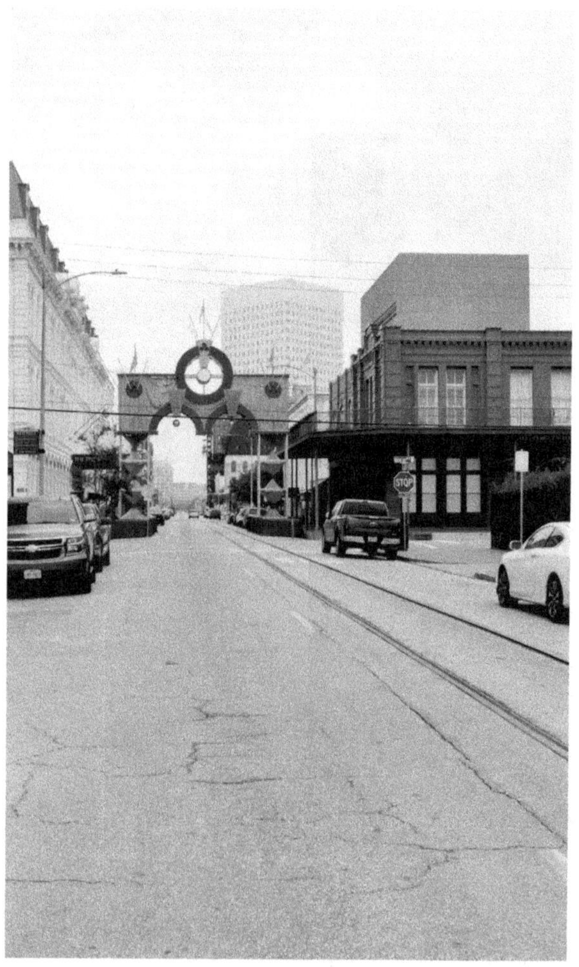

LET THE OCEAN...

Let the ocean be your mentor; it knows how to weather storms and still sparkle.

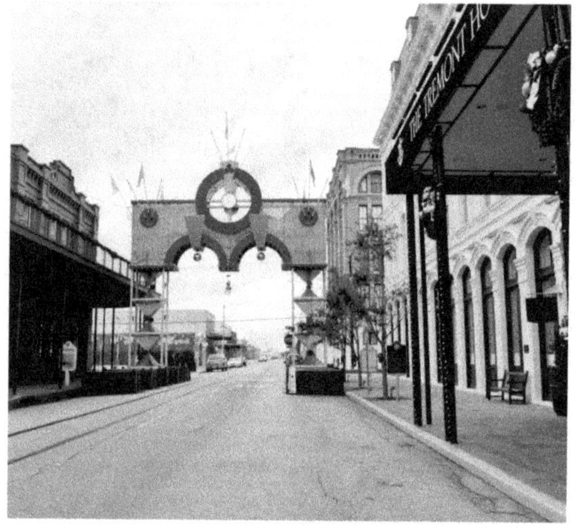

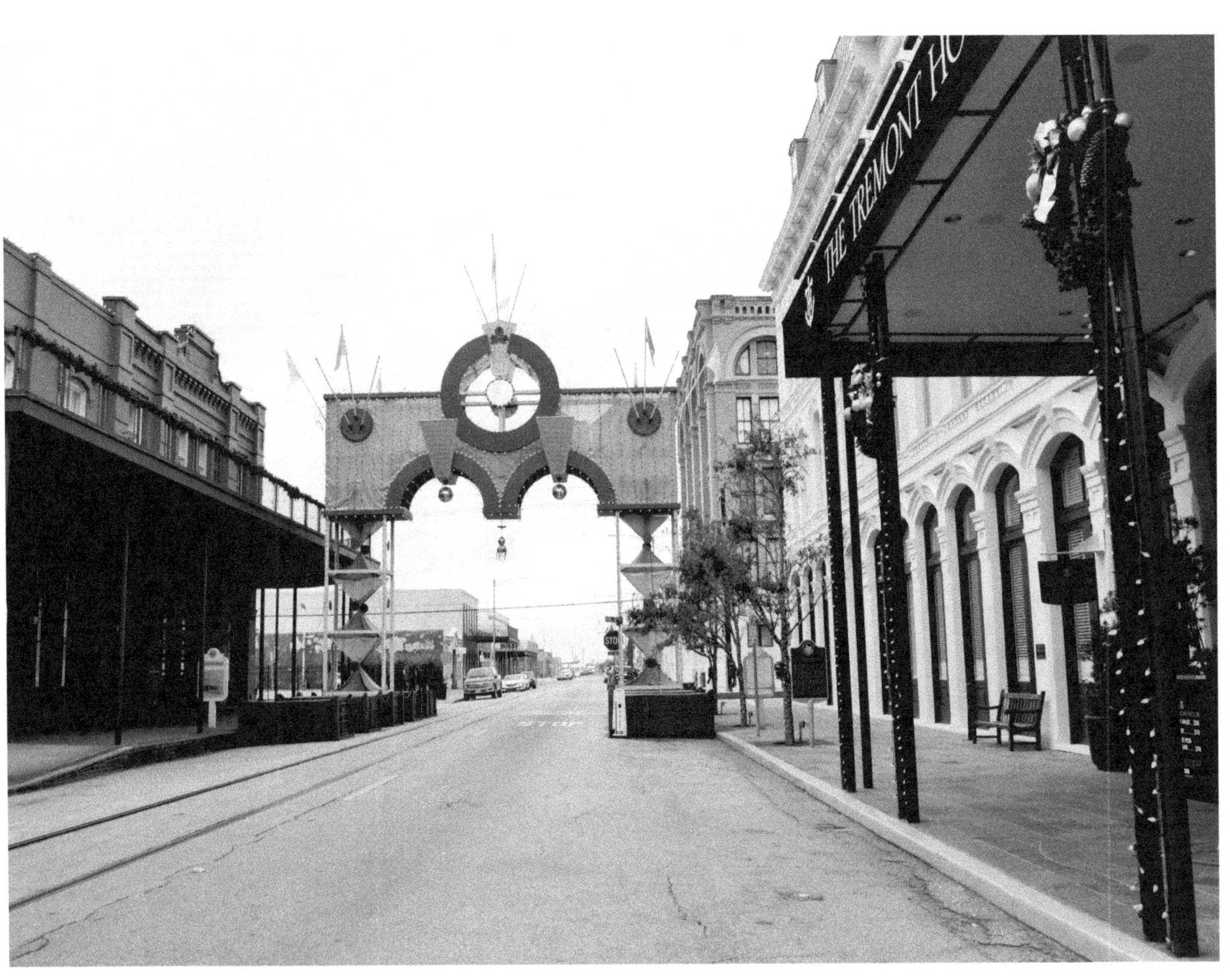

Saltwater heals everything – tears, sweat, and the wounds of the so

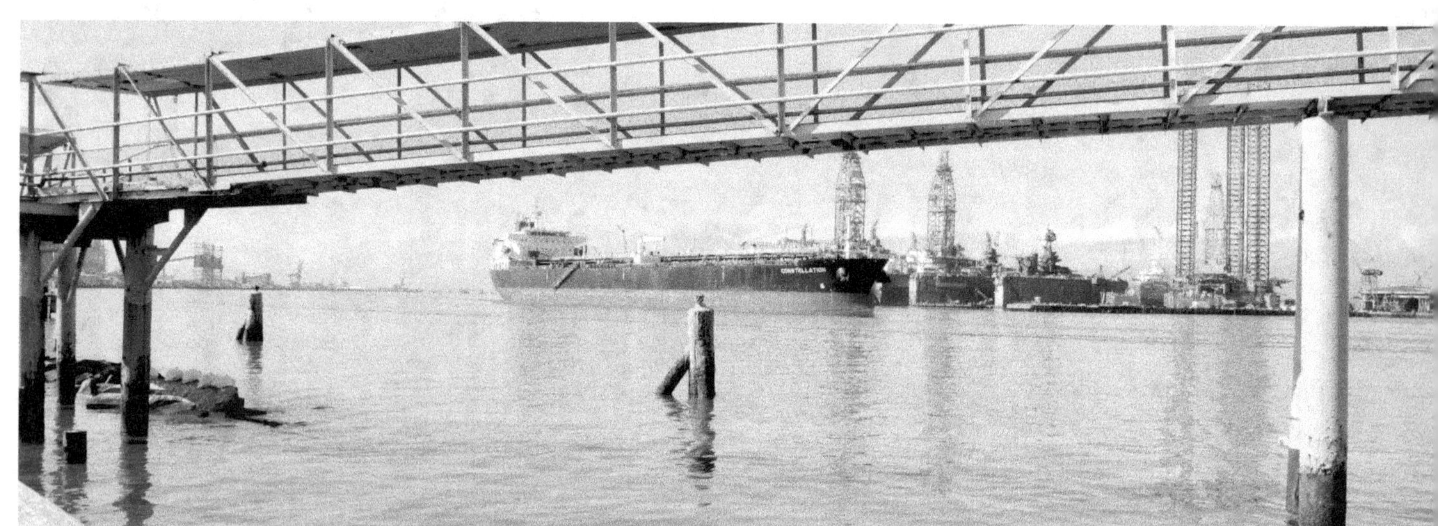

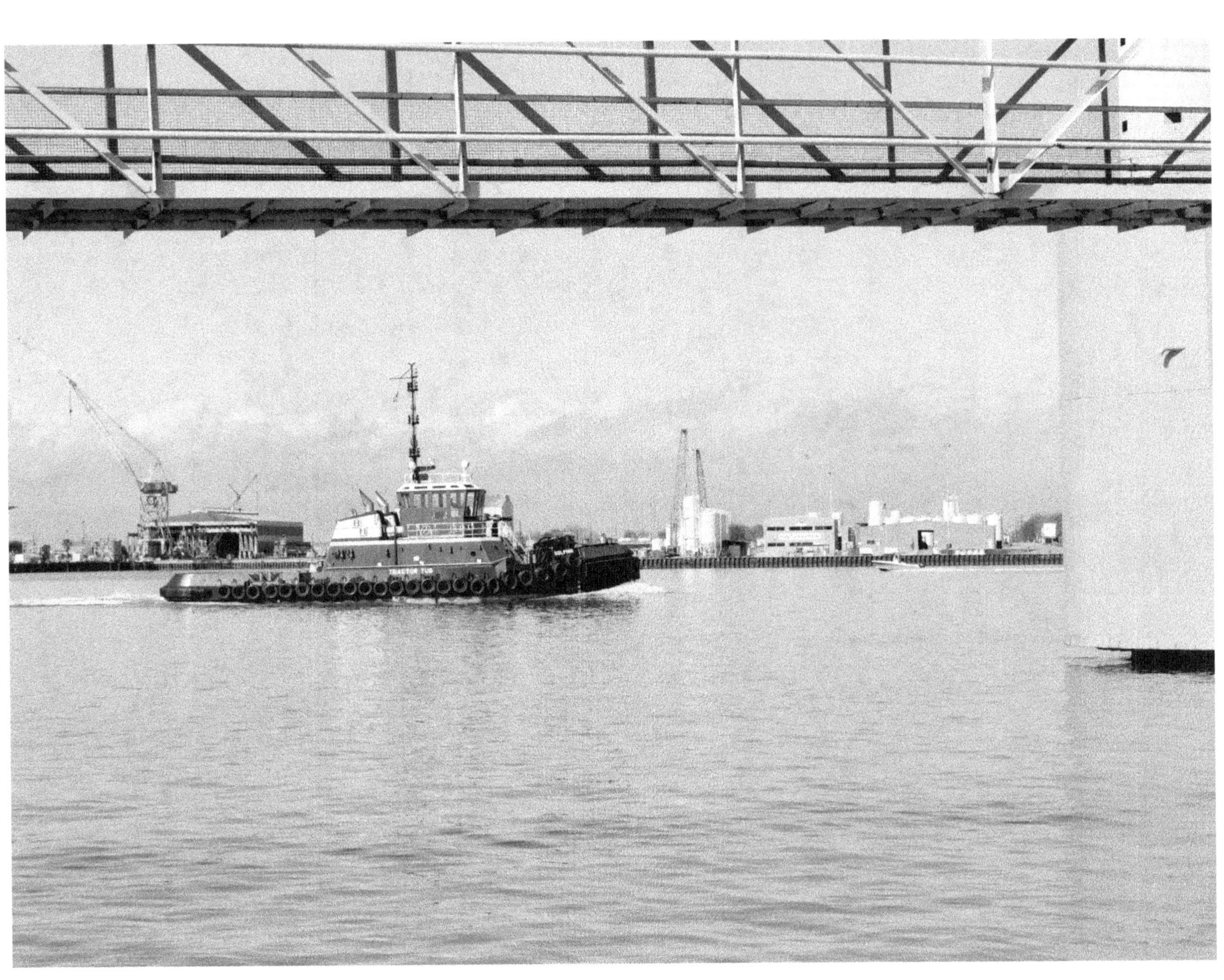

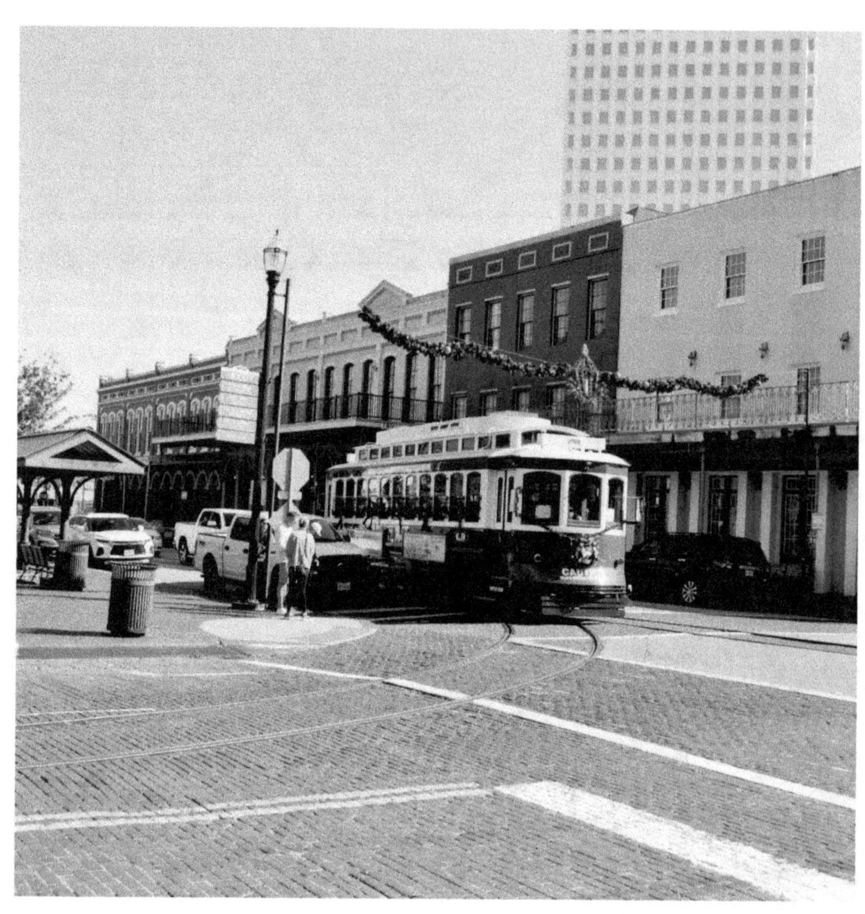

LIFE...

Life is a beach ball – catch it with a smile and play along.

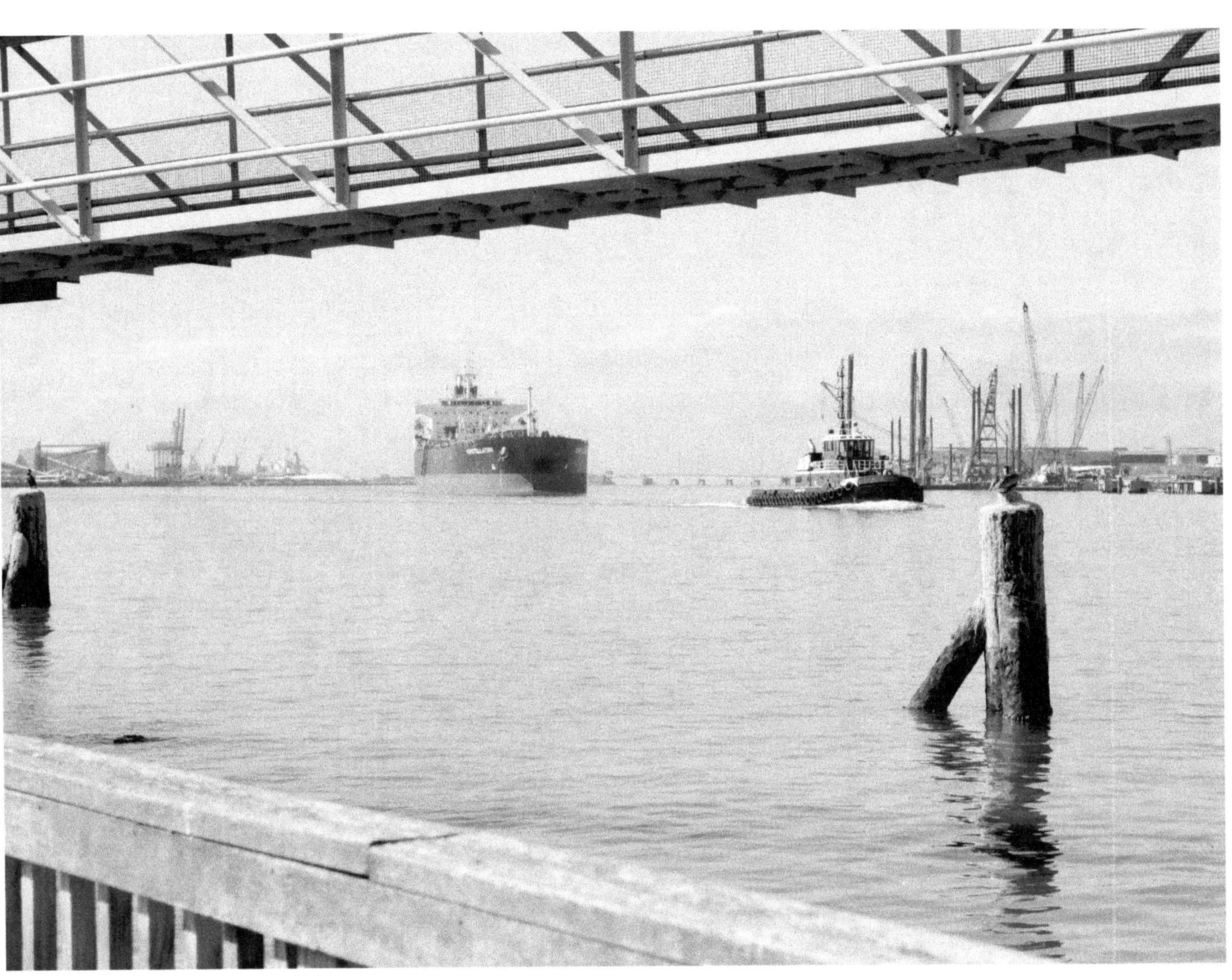

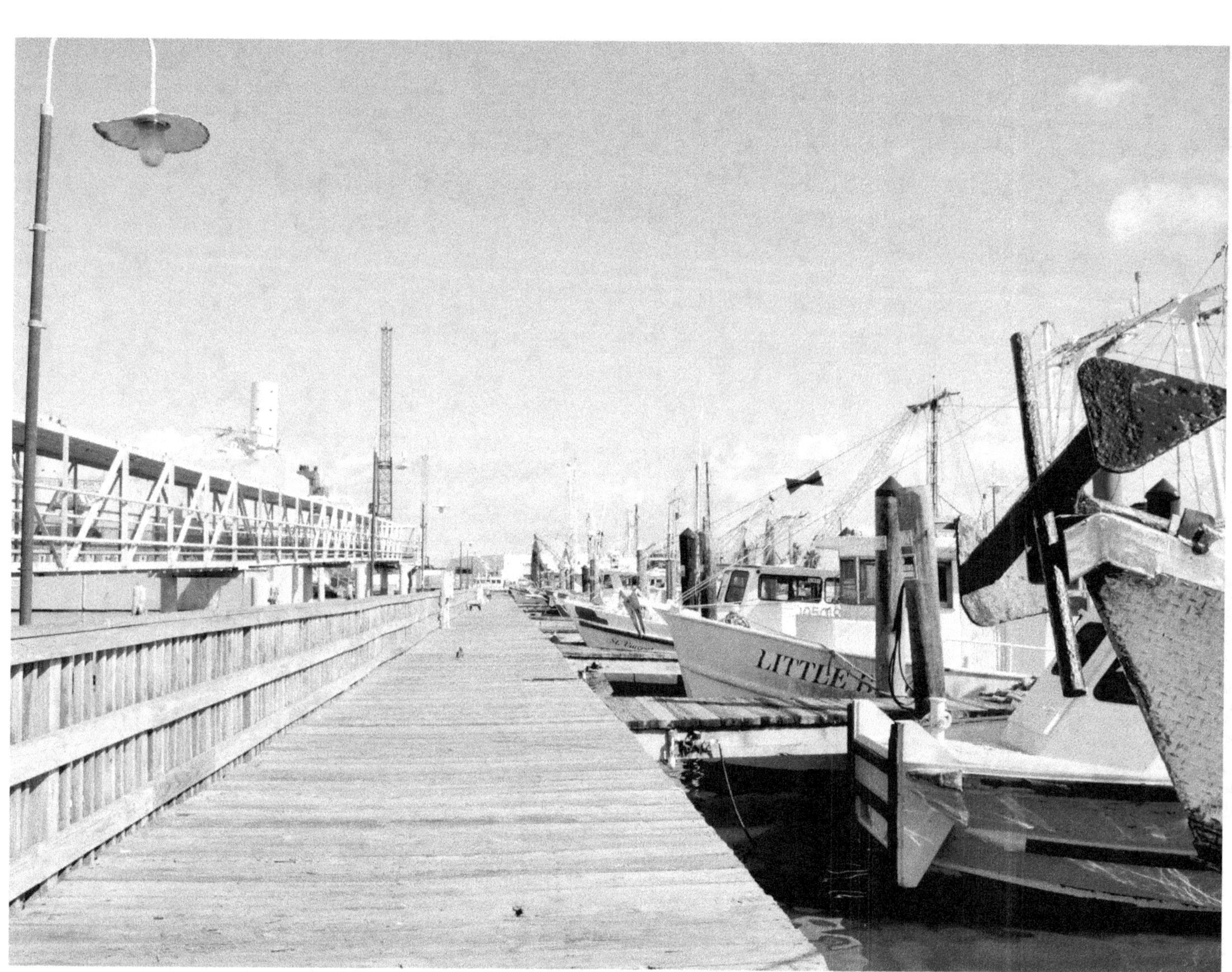

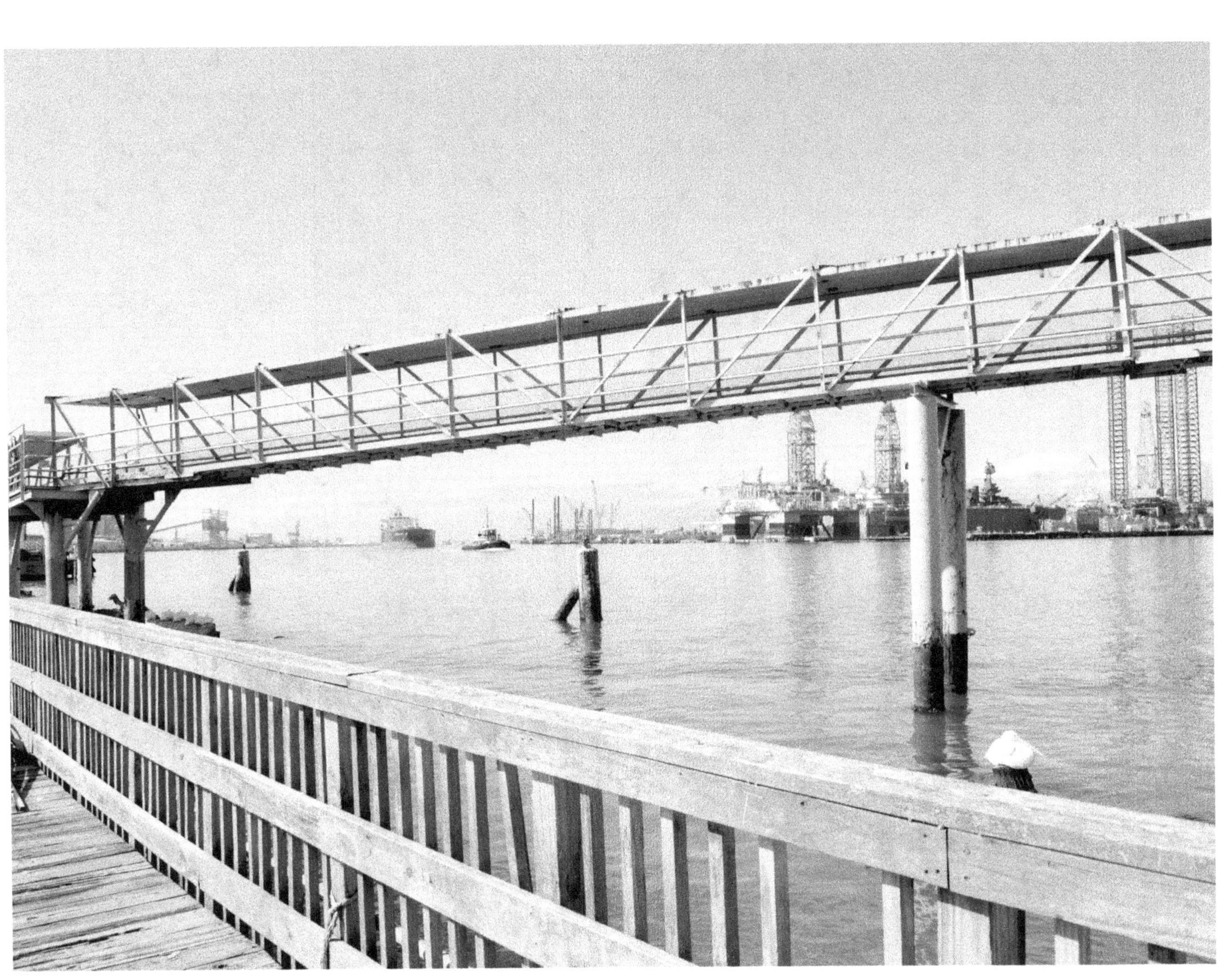

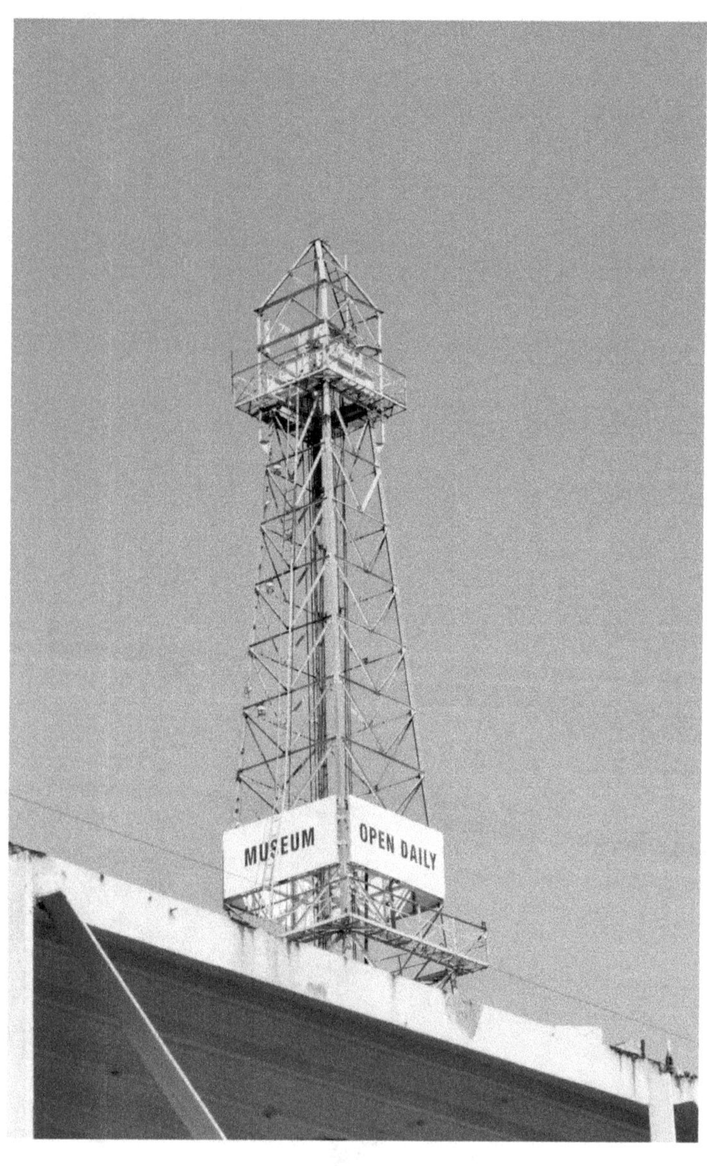

MEMORIES...

Sandcastles are fleeting, but the memories we build are everlasting.

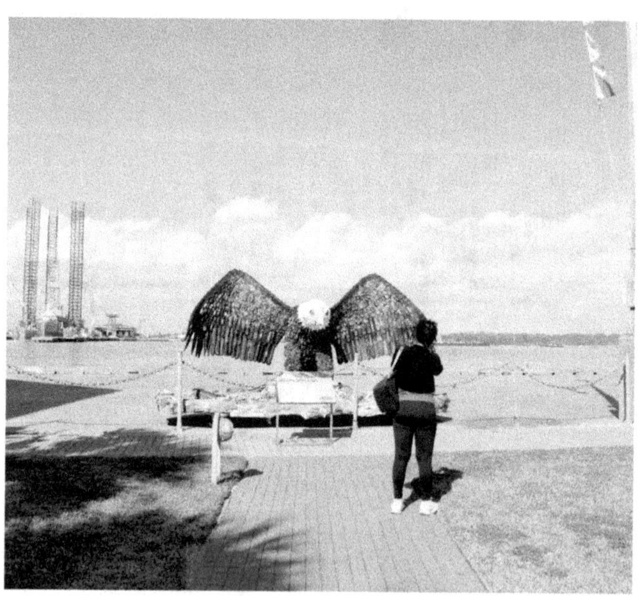

Step into the sunlight of possibility and leave footprints of courage in the sands of time

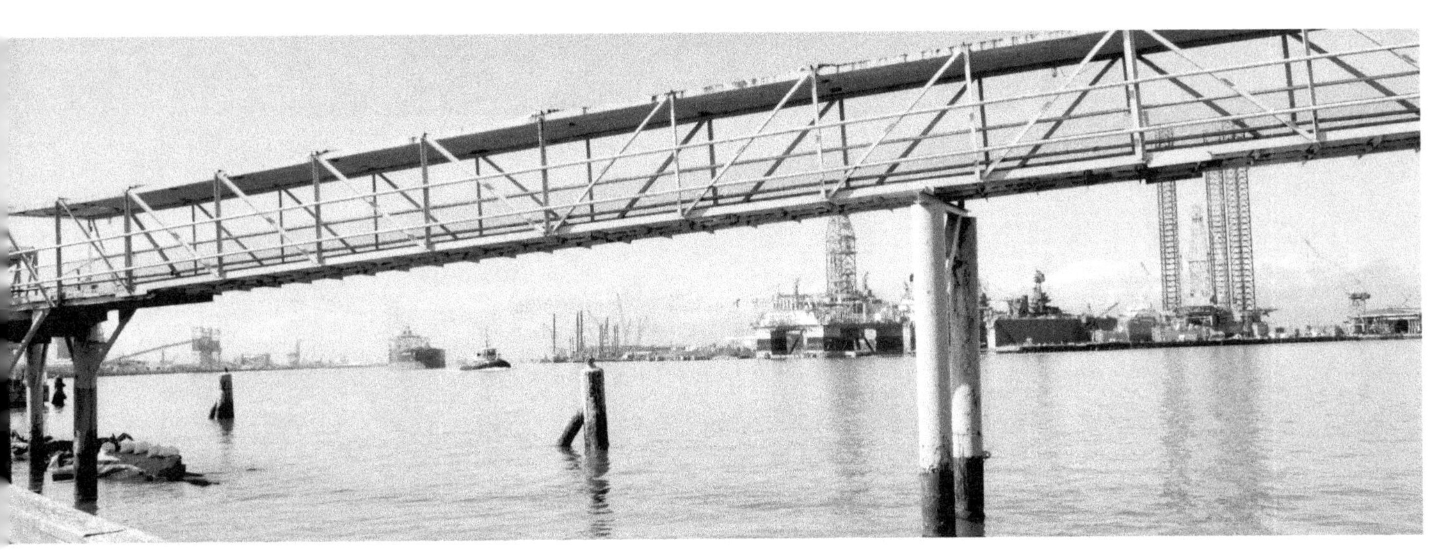

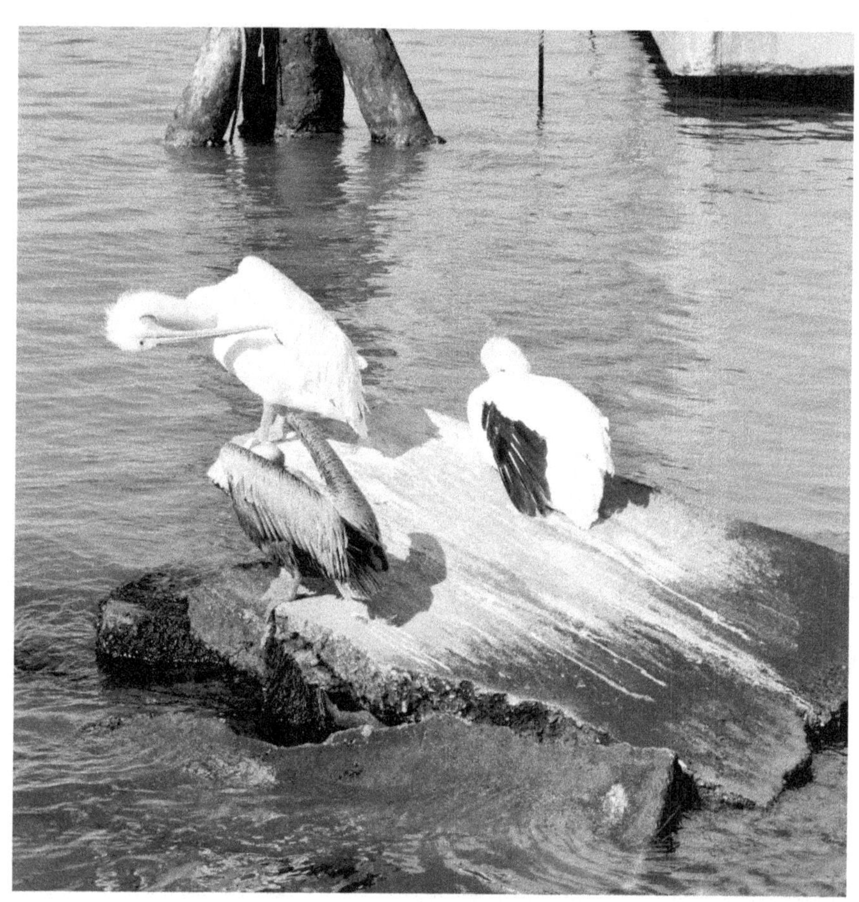

BEACH

*Beach days are therapy for the soul, prescribed by the tides and administered
by the sun.*

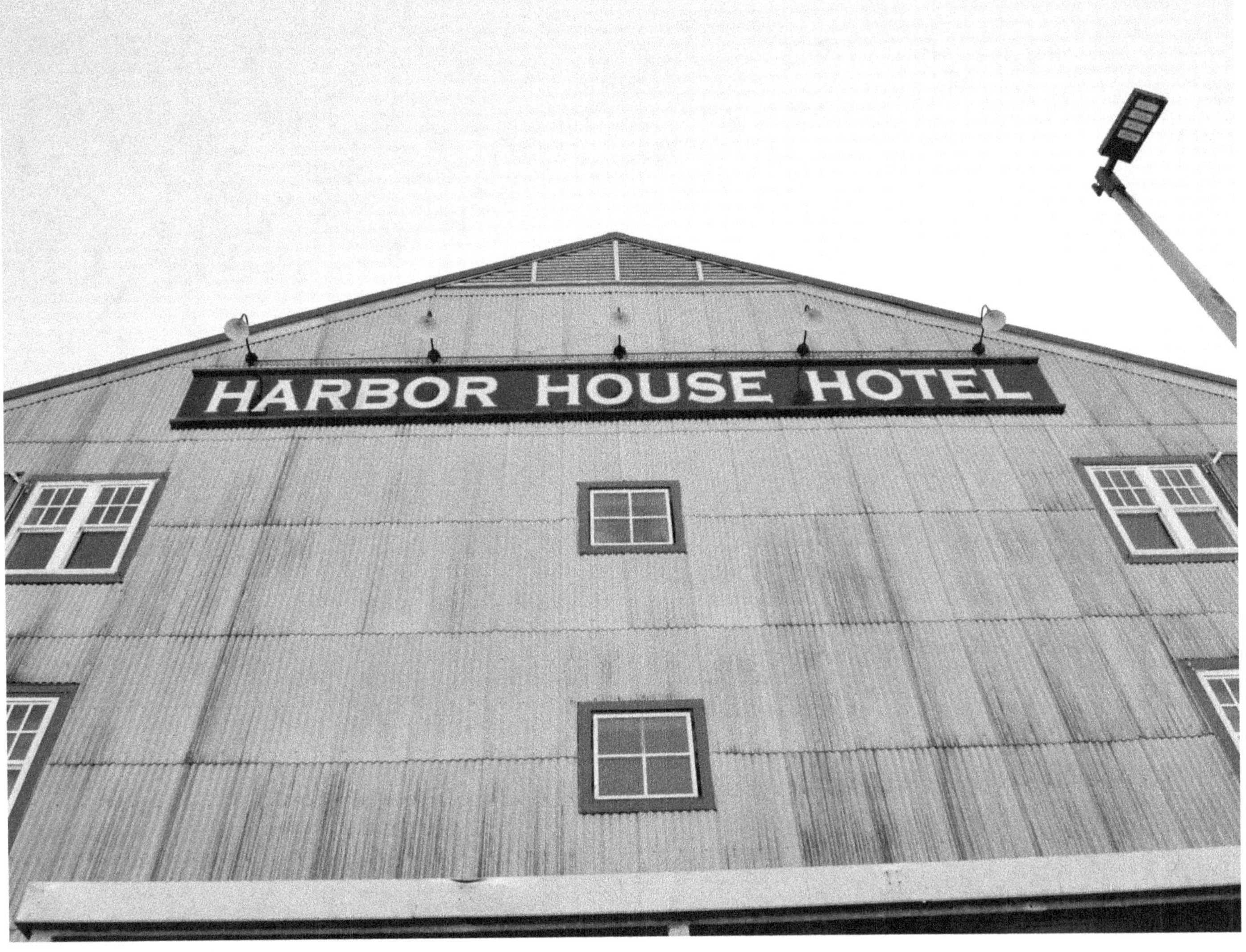

HARBOR HOUSE HOTEL

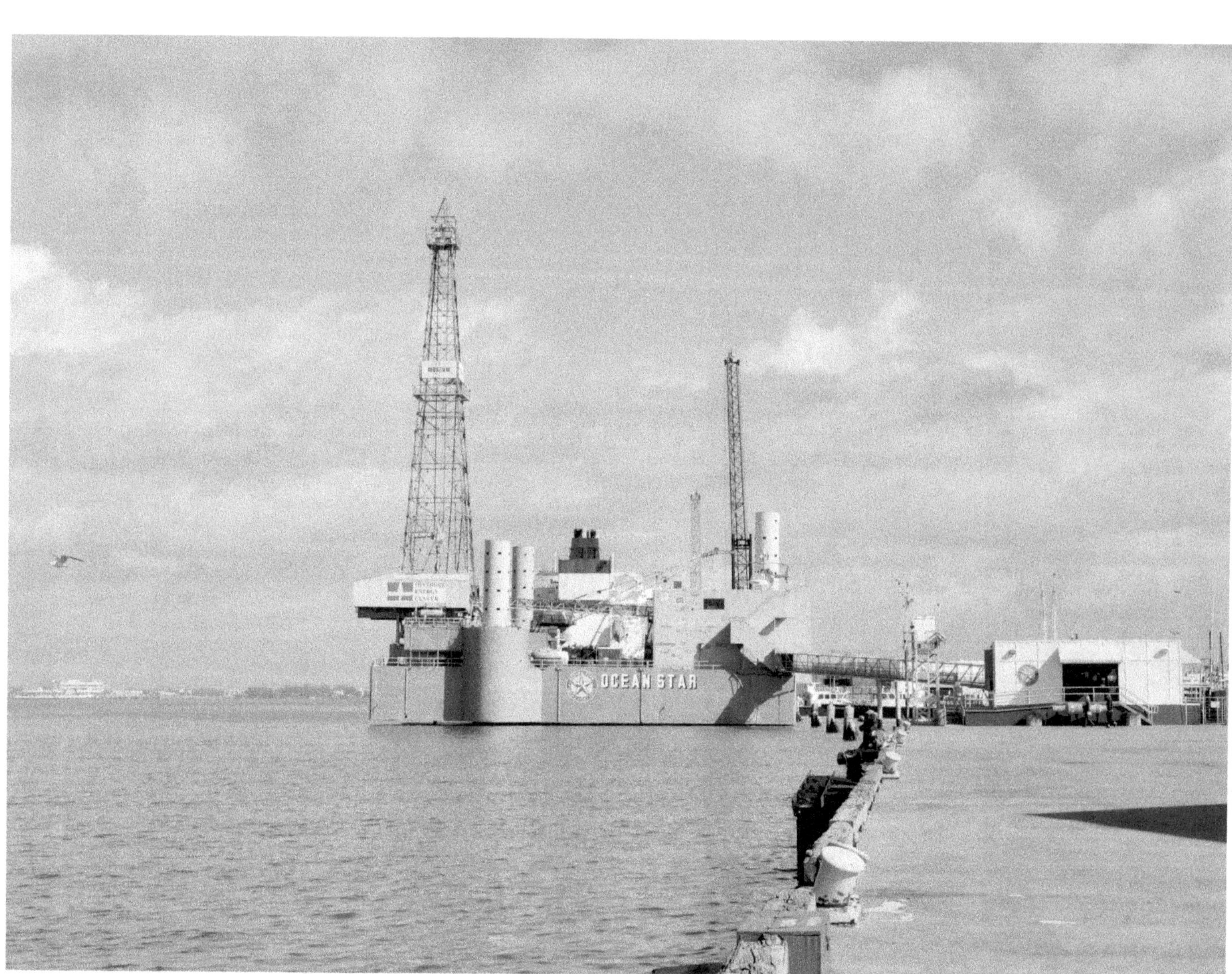

OCEAN STAR

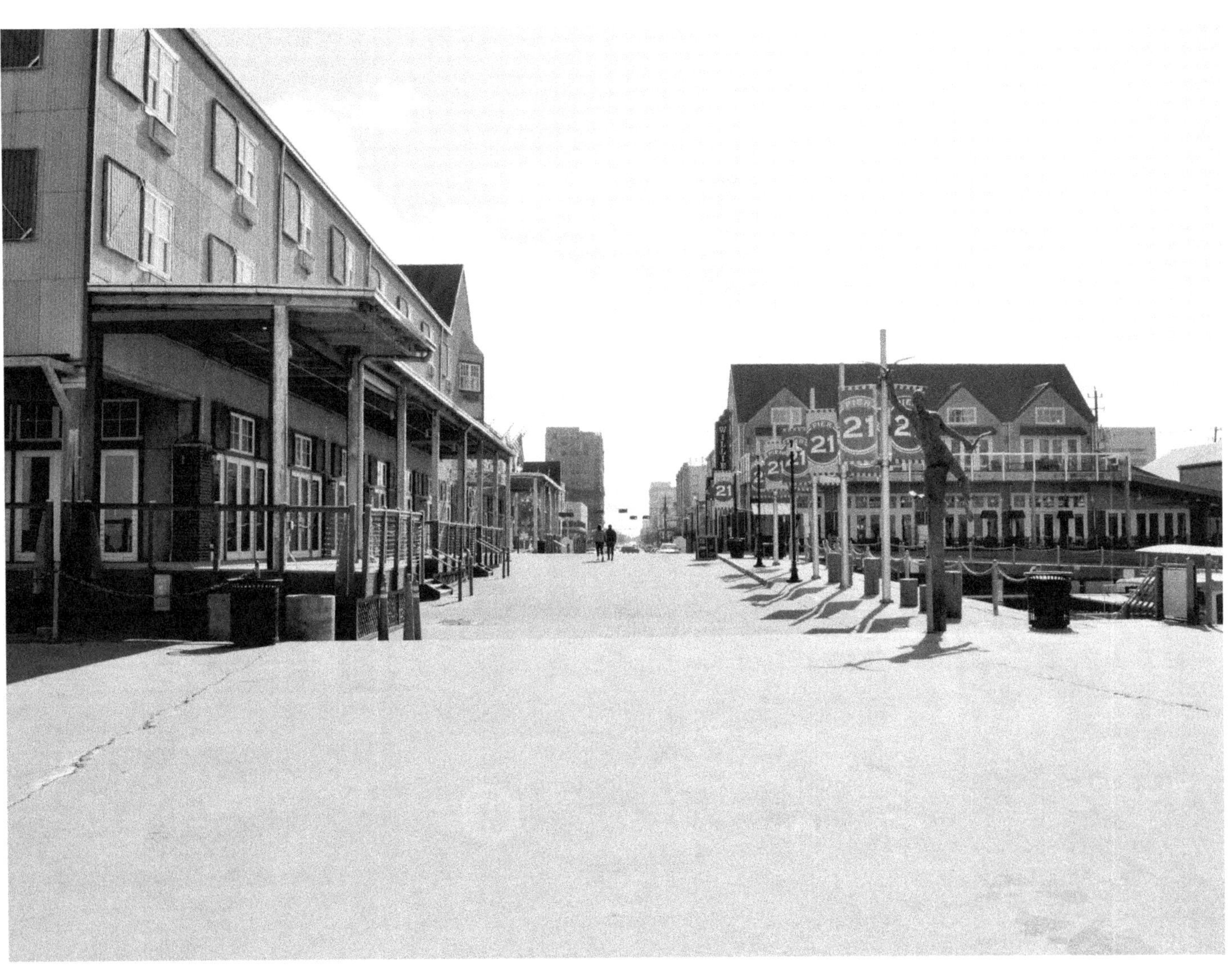

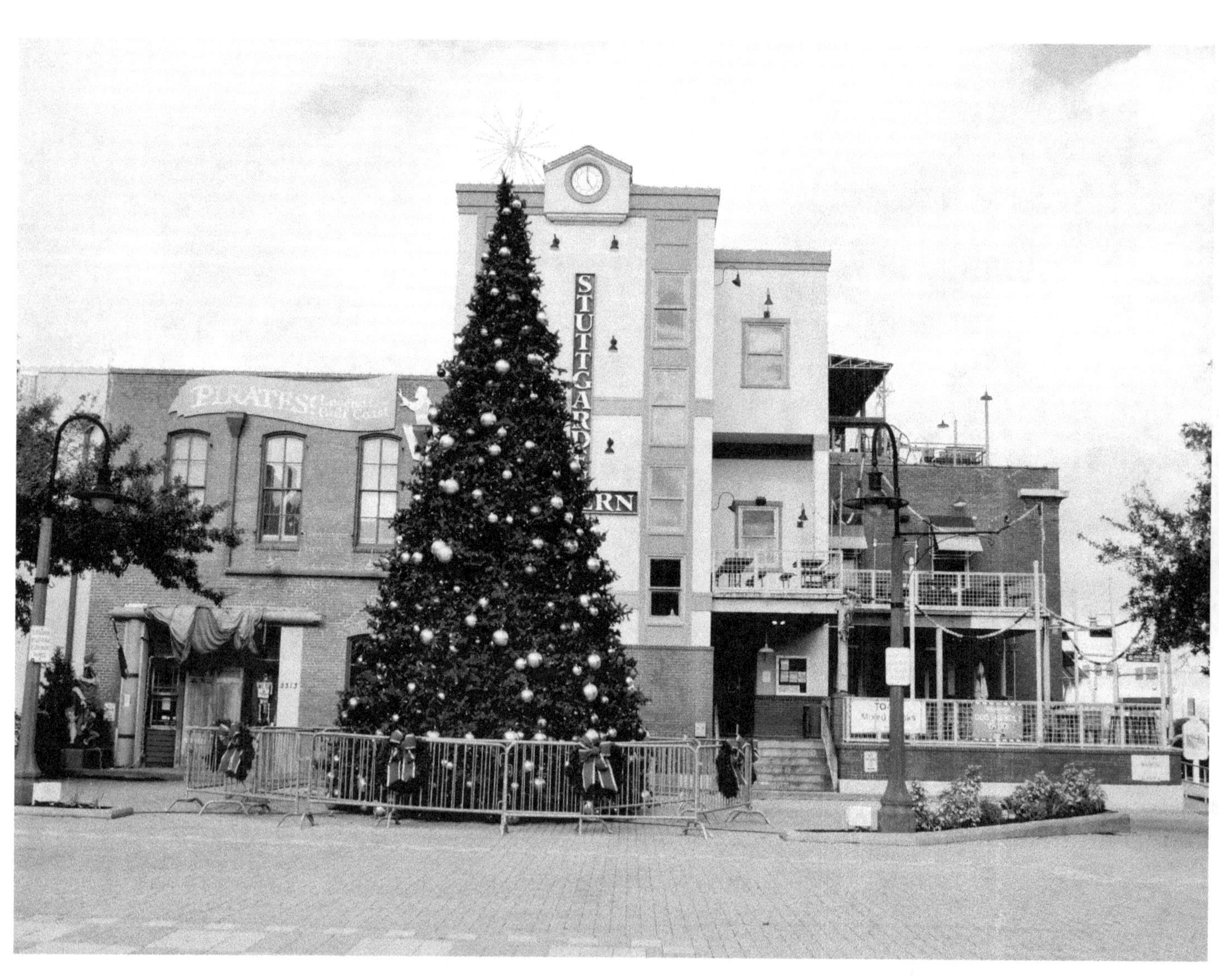

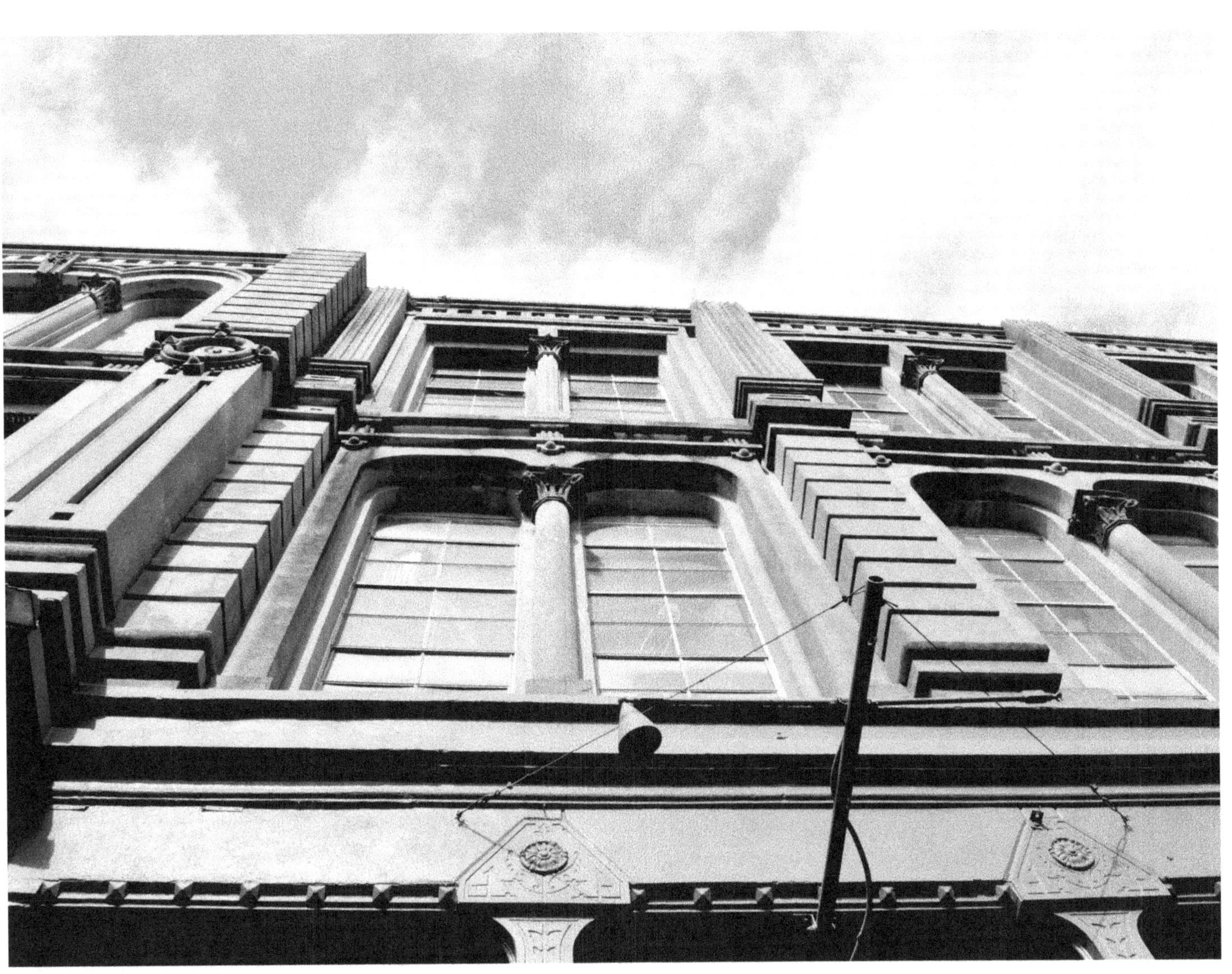

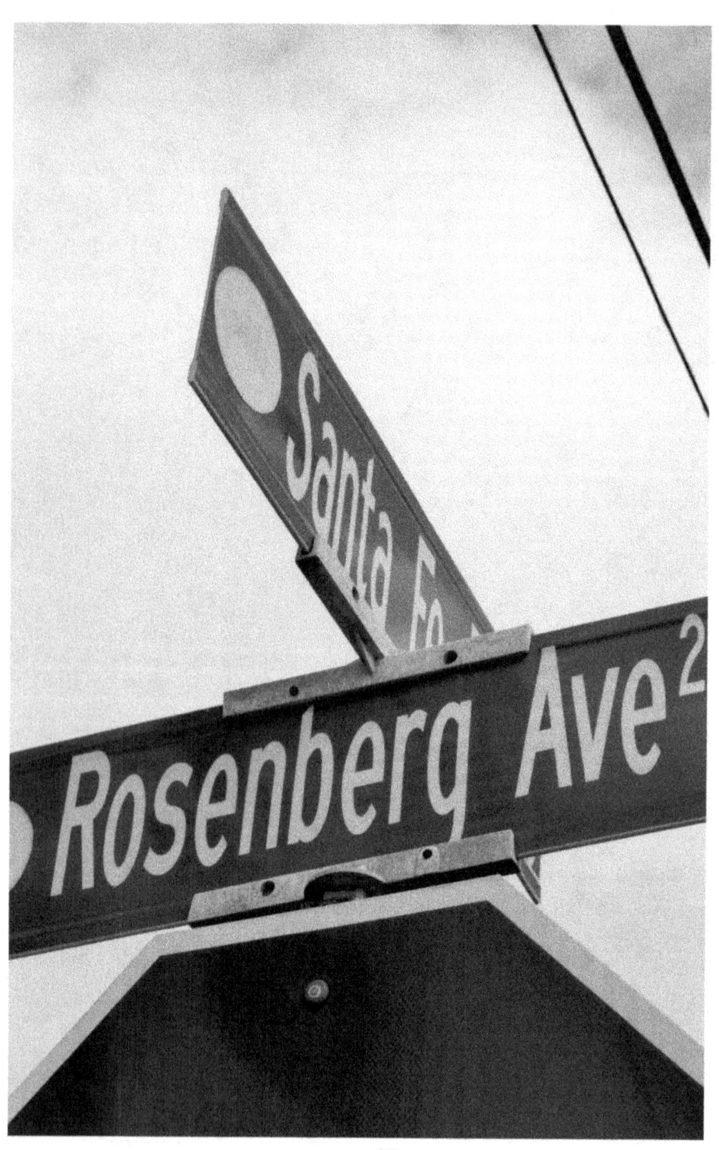

LOVE...

Anchored by love, buoyed by hope – sail through life with the wind of positivity.

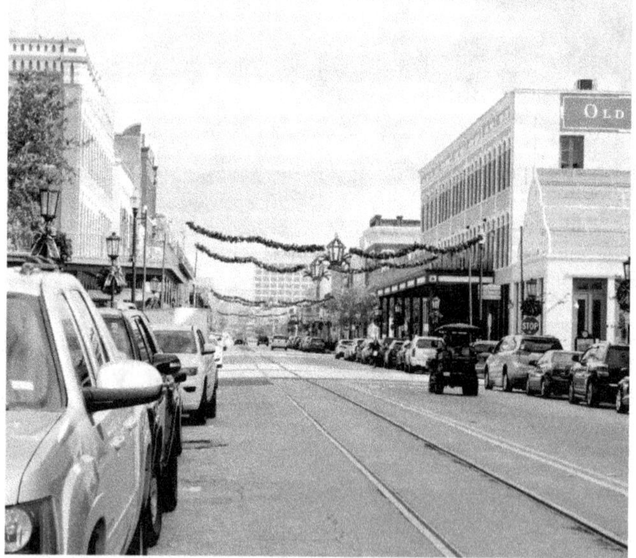

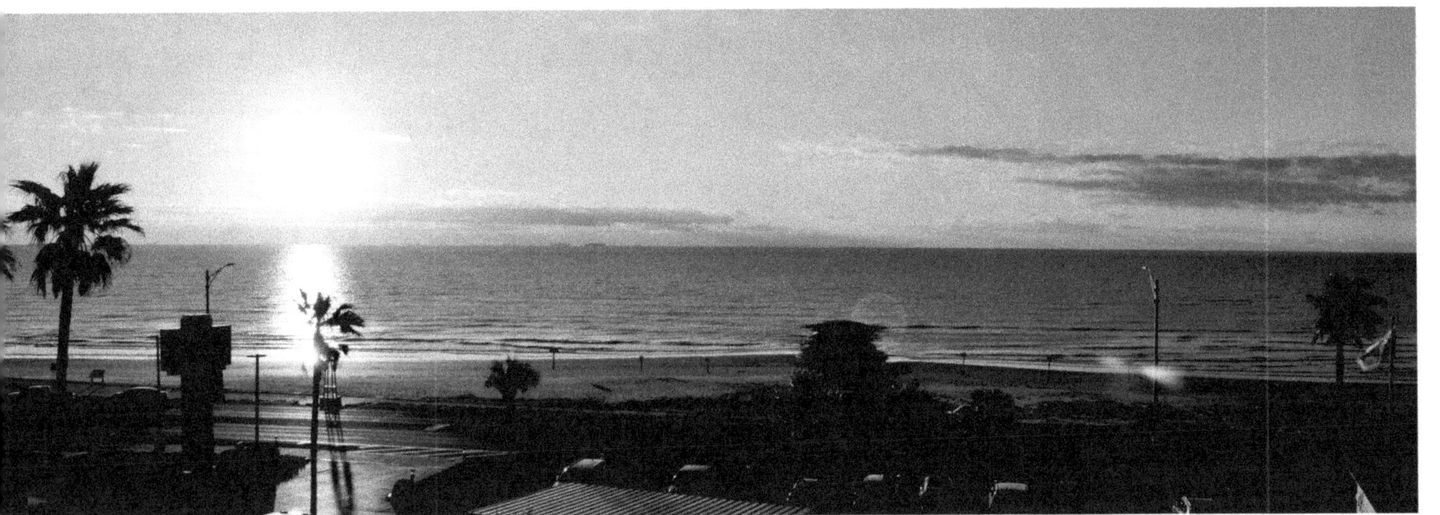

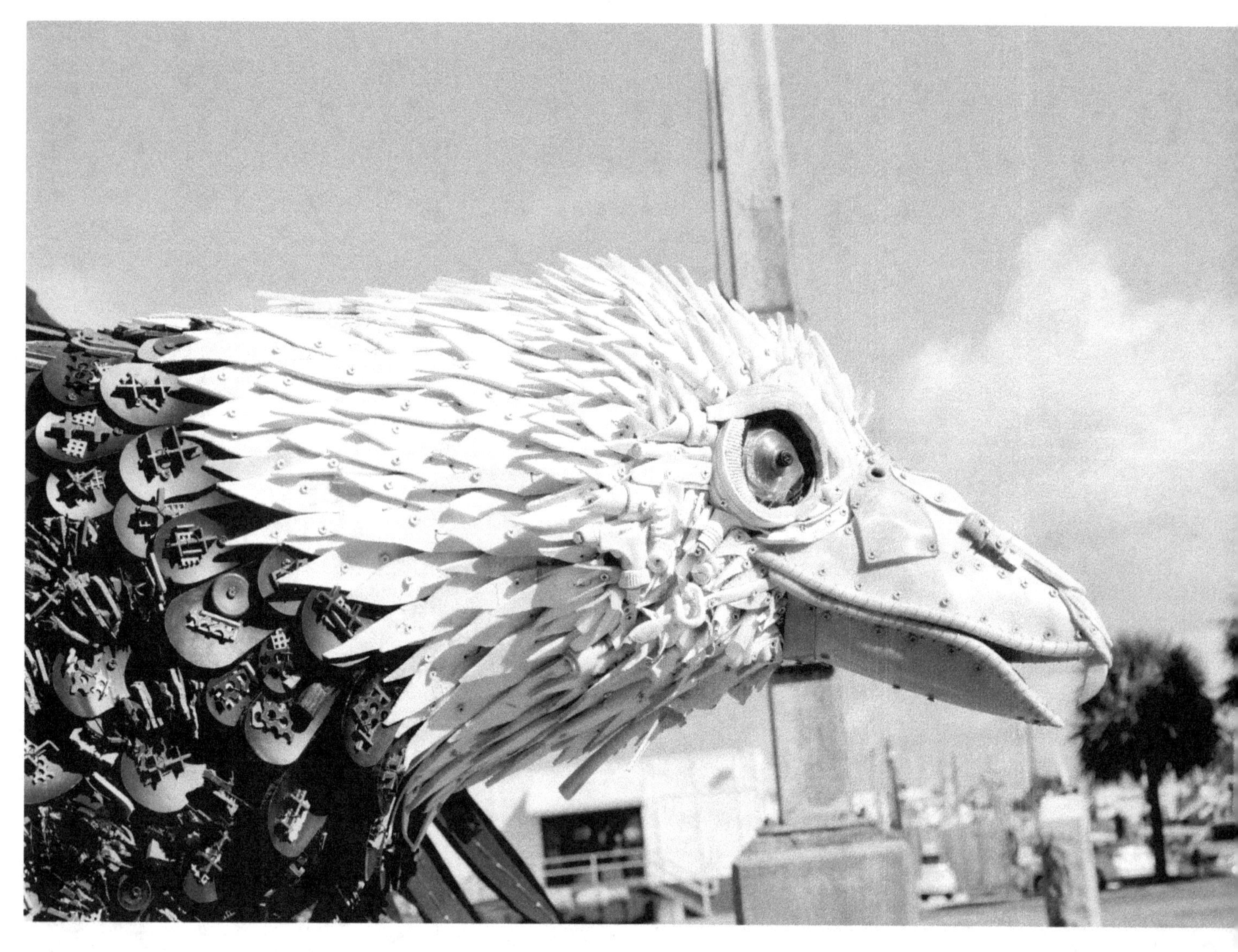

Galveston Texas
By
Francisco Jose Zangerolame